AMAZON FBA MADE SIMPLE

[3 in 1 Compilation]

How to Find & Evaluate Suppliers, Increase Your Amazon Sales, and Launch a Million Dollar Ecommerce Brand

Red Mikhail

A Note About the Bundle:

This is a compilation of 3 books within the Amazon FBA Business Series.

This bundle includes the following:

FBA PRODUCT SOURCING BLUEPRINT – to help you find and evaluate the best suppliers. [Page 3]

AMAZON FBA SALES BOOST – to help you double or even triple your Amazon sales. [Page 86]

MILLION DOLLAR ECOMMERCE – to help you create an ecommerce brand that generates 6-7 figures per year. [Page 190]

I hope that this bundle serves you well.

All the best,

Red

FBA

PRODUCT SOURCING

BLUEPRINT

How to Find, Evaluate, and Hire the Best Suppliers
at the Best Prices for Your Fulfillment by Amazon Business

Red Mikhail

TABLE OF CONTENTS

Introduction

Welcome to Part 4 of the Amazon FBA Business Series – FBA Product Sourcing Blueprint. In part 1, we talked about the AMAZON FBA business in general and how a beginner can get started even without huge capital or experience. In part 2, we discussed the importance of product research and how you can find products that has a higher chance of being profitable. And in part 3, we discussed the role of keyword research on your FBA business and I taught you the best strategies for doing keyword research without using any paid tools.

In this book, we are going to focus our attention on finding suppliers, negotiating the best prices, shipping our products and making sure that it reaches Amazon's fulfillment center so we can start selling it on Amazon.com as soon as possible.

In case you haven't got the chance to read part 1 to part 3 yet, I would highly recommend that you start with them as they would serve as great foundational knowledge for the lessons to come. They are all available in eBook, paperback and audiobook format.

So, who is this book for?

It is for people who already have a basic idea of how ecommerce works and someone who already have a product in mind. We won't discuss product research in this book so you might want to get a handle of that part first if you don't have any idea what product to sell yet. However, if you already have something in mind, then this book will be crucial to your FBA journey.

Finding product suppliers is where most people get stuck. It's understandable because this is where you put your money where your mouth is. This is the part where you invest in product samples and your first order.

Depending on the product you chose, that would likely cost between $500-$5,000.

So yeah, your business isn't just an idea anymore – your physical product now makes it real.

Now, I don't want you to be afraid of the process because it can be pretty simple as long as you follow the guidelines and steps that I'm going to discuss in this book.

Here's an overview of the whole process.

Chapter 1 - Researching Suppliers

First, I'll show you how to research the best suppliers and I'll give you 5 of the best ways to find quality suppliers that won't take advantage of you.

What criteria do you have to follow so you can pick the best suppliers for your product? I will reveal all of that in this chapter.

Chapter 2 – Hiring the Best Suppliers

Next, I'll teach you how to veto your suppliers so you know that you're only dealing with legit ones. You won't want to get scammed for $5,000 for your first order, don't you? In this chapter, I'll show you how to make the initial contact and what questions to ask to know if they are a legit manufacturer or not.

Chapter 3 – Ordering Units, Negotiating for the Best Prices and the Shipping Process Explained

In this chapter, I'll give you the steps that you need to take to make sure that you are making the right order for your product. I will also give you a checklist of things to remember before you finalize your order. This will also help you avoid losing money which most first-time sellers do.

In this chapter, I'll also teach you how to negotiate for the best prices where you'll both come out feeling like a winner.

In addition, we'll also discuss the all-too confusing shipping process where most people get into a lot of trouble for.

What's the process of shipping from your supplier to your address or Amazon's fulfillment center? What you do actually do each time you have a shipment ready to sell on AMAZON FBA? Follow my lead and I guarantee that you'll have a much seamless process of getting your products to Amazon's fulfillment center.

Chapter 4 – Barcodes and FBA Fees Demystified

In chapter 4, we'll talk about how to set up your Barcodes, how they work, and how to calculate your FBA fees.

And lastly, in **Chapter 5**, we'll discuss the best **Practices of the Most Profitable Ecommerce Business Owners** as it relates to finding the best suppliers, dealing with suppliers and making the shipping process as seamless as possible.

Think of these as your personal guidelines to follow so you won't lose your shirt in this business.

The Importance of Finding Great Suppliers

Finding great suppliers isn't exactly rocket science. It takes a bit of practice to master and you'll still probably make some mistakes even if you follow every single thing I say in this book. And that's perfectly fine. In fact, you should expect this process to be hard. If it's easy, then everybody would do it and this business wouldn't be as profitable as it is. The good news is finding great suppliers is a learnable skill. If you're willing to make an investment in time, money and effort – then I don't see any reason why you won't succeed. With the right product and the right supplier, you can build a business that would still exist 3,5 10 or even 20 years from now. A business that will feed your family, pay for your vacations, and buy your heart's desire. But then again, it's not as easy as ABC. If you're willing to go through learning pains, then I have a feeling that you will be one of the people who will still be thriving in this business years from now.

I hope I didn't scare you into quitting! Ha ha.
If I did, then this business is probably not for you.

If you're still here, then allow me to show you the way.

Chapter 1
Researching Suppliers

Finding the right supplier is where we separate the boys from the men, the wantrepreneur to the entrepreneur, and the wannabe boss to the serious business owner. Why? Because it's the part where you put your money where your mouth is. Now it's time to actually invest a few hundred dollars to a few thousand dollars for your first inventory. So, we want to make this right and make sure that we don't make the all too common mistakes most newbie ecommerce sellers make.

The Dangers of Choosing the Wrong Supplier

1 – You'll lose time & money

If you get the wrong supplier, then you'll have a really miserable time because you'll probably lose money. You can pick an unreliable supplier and extend the process for months and months with nothing to show for it. You may pick a supplier who's just outsourcing the manufacturing to other bigger suppliers. You may get lots of additional hidden costs that you're not expecting. Heck, you may even get scammed by a supplier. All of these things may happen and you need to be 100% sure that you are dealing with a legit supplier.

2 – You'll quit

More painful than losing time & money is the act of quitting the business.
After all the work you've put in so far, the capital you invested and the effort you put working on the business may be for nothing if you quit because you lost your shirt and you lost trust in the process because of dealing with the wrong supplier.

Trust me, I know dozens of new sellers who quitted because of how painful the experience has been dealing with the wrong supplier.

So, what do you need to check to be sure that you are only working with a legit supplier?

What to Look for in a Supplier

1 – Legit Operations

First, check if the company has a website (and they should have one!). If you're using Alibaba, HKTDC or the other platforms that I'm going to show you later, they should have a company profile that shows different aspects of their business.

Stuff like the type of business they have, their company address, trademarks, product certifications, number of employees and the year they were established.

Business Type	Manufacturer, Other		Country / Region	Guangdong, China	✓
Main Products	Wireless Microphone, Speaker, Wired Microphone		Total Employees	11 - 50 People	
Total Annual Revenue	Below US$1 Million		Year Established	2016	✓
Certifications			Product Certifications(6)	CE, CE, ROHS, CE, CE, ROHS	✓
Patents(1)	wireless microphone(87)	✓	Trademarks(1)	BAOBAOMI	✓
Main Markets	Southeast Asia 26.00% North America 10.00% Domestic Market 10.00%				

[Image 1.1]

It's not that hard to find these details and it's definitely worth the time researching them and confirming if these are true.

What I like about using Alibaba, HKTDC, TTNET and other platforms is their verification process. They have a reputation to uphold and they won't just allow any supplier to sell on their platform.

2 – Client Feedback and Online Reputation

Another thing to look at are their client's feedback and their online reputation in general. For client feedback, read the reviews they are getting on their profile or product pages. The more positive feedback they have, the better.

Also, Google their company and make sure that they do not have any pending cases or complaints. Not all companies will have 100% happy customers but you should try to find a company that has zero bad records if possible.

3 – Years in Business

You can also find the number of years they have been operating as a manufacturer. This is important because you want someone who already knows the entire process of how all of this works. You don't want to be their guinea pig as they try to navigate starting their own manufacturing business. As a rule of thumb, I only work with manufacturers who already has at least 4-5 years of experience in the business.

4 – Customization Availability

Make sure that they allow product customization as well. If you are doing a private label product, it is crucial that you have some kind of differentiation from your competition. Most manufacturers will allow branding but that's just the first step.

Can they offer different colors? Can they create a different mold? Are they open to changing some aspects of the product so it can match your vision?

Work with someone who's open to all of these things because you cannot dominate FBA if you're just selling a "me too" products without any differentiation at all.

5 – Product Availability

This is an obvious one. Always confirm to them if they can make that specific product and if they have the available resources to do so. Some companies will say yes but will then outsource to other manufacturers. Never ever deal with a manufacturer who has to pass the product creation part to other companies. You have to make sure that you're dealing with them directly so you'll have full control of what the final product may look like.

6 – The Numbers Make Sense

We are doing this because we want to make money. So, the numbers have to make sense. If you are getting the product at $3 each, you must be able to sell it for at least $15 on Amazon. Anything less would probably result in a net loss.

To avoid losing money, I always follow the 5X Rule.

The 5X rule states that you must be able to sell the product at 5x its manufacturing cost so you can at least break even.

There are other expenses that you have to think about like shipping, FBA fees, selling fees, and product inspection (which we'll talk about in chapter 4). All of those things may add up and following the 5X rule puts you on a safe side and allows you to at the very least, breakeven. Obviously, it's all different and it will still depend on the product that you are selling. But as a general rule, I just go to Amazon first and compared what price is the product selling at and how much does it cost per quantity to produce.

For example, if this BBQ gloves sell for $3.25 in Alibaba, then I must be able to sell it on Amazon for at least $16.25. (please see images 1.2 and 1.3 for reference)

(Image 1.2)

(Image 1.3)

The key here is to find a product on Amazon that is as close to the one you are looking at on Alibaba or other manufacturing platforms.

7 – Willingness to Negotiate

You'll never really know this until later in the process. For now, just keep in mind that pro-sellers will always be willing to negotiate a win-win deal so you guys can make a long-term business relationship.

8 – Badges

Most manufacturing platforms will have some kind of badge that shows social proof and the legitimacy of the manufacturing company.

Later, I'll explain them in detail and I'll show you the most important ones to look at.

9 – Response Time & Quality of Response

Another important thing is their response time. Are they getting back to you within 12-48 hours or do they usually take 4-5 days to reply?

I only deal with suppliers who always get back to me within 48 hours.

Now, it's not just enough that they get back to me on time. It's also important that their response actually answers my questions and concerns.

10 – Lead Time & Shipping Time

Lead time is the number of days or weeks it takes for them to finish manufacturing your product. Setting the right expectation and communication is the key here. If they say that they need at least 4 weeks to manufacture your Christmas related product and its already November 20, then you probably won't make the cut since you still have to do the shipping which usually takes 7-45 days depending on the option you choose. By the time your Christmas related product appears on your Amazon store, it would already be too late since it'll most likely already be January.

Remember this simple formula, **lead time + shipping time = product availability date on Amazon.**

11 – Payment Options

Make sure that they have lots of payment options available. I never ever do Western Union since it can get sketchy when it comes to tracking that payment.

For a safer payment, you can do VISA, Mastercard, Apple Pay, and PayPal instead.

Trade Assurance protects your Alibaba.com orders

Payments: VISA T/T Online Transfer Pay WesternUnion WU

Alibaba.com Logistics   Inspection Solutions   Production View   One-Stop Service

(Image 1.4)

12 – They Already Deal with Other FBA Sellers

It boggles my mind that new FBA sellers don't ask their supplier if they already have some kind of experience with other FBA sellers. Asking this simple question will save you lots of time and headache in the process. If you're dealing with a company that already manufactures and ships for other FBA sellers, then you're in luck because they already know what to do and they can also educate you on how all of these works.

This is not a requirement per se, but dealing with a manufacturer with lots of experience with other FBA sellers will result in a more likely positive experience for you.

****

In the next part of this chapter (as well as in chapters 2 & 3), I'll show you how you can apply all of these and how you can use these 12 criteria when searching for a supplier. I'll give you some examples, screenshots, templates and an explanation on why I picked a specific supplier as well.

5 WAYS TO FIND A SUPPLIER

A - Google Search

I know this is pretty obvious, but I recommend that this is where you start. Just search on Google and find potential suppliers that matches your product.

Here are some examples + keyword terms to use:

1 – Product Name + Supplier

Just type your product name + add the word "supplier" in it.

boardmarker supplier

(Image 1.5)

You will likely see lots of websites offering the product you are looking for. Sometimes, they will be independent website or the supplier's website. Other times, you will see supplier listings from Alibaba, HKTDC and other big manufacturing platforms.

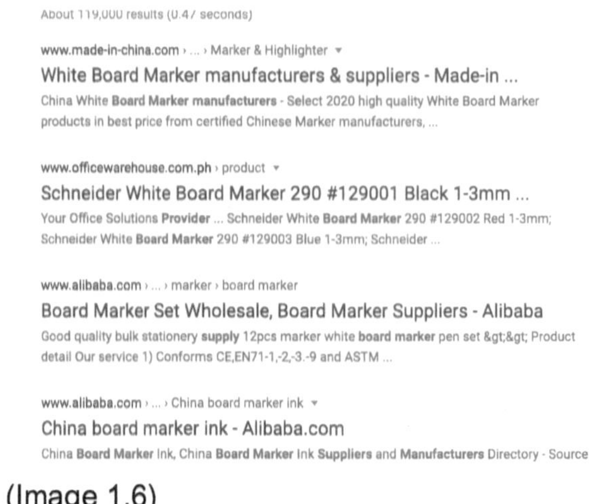

(Image 1.6)

2 – Product Name + Private Label

If you are looking to sell a private label product with your own brand, you can also use the search term "private label" after your product name.

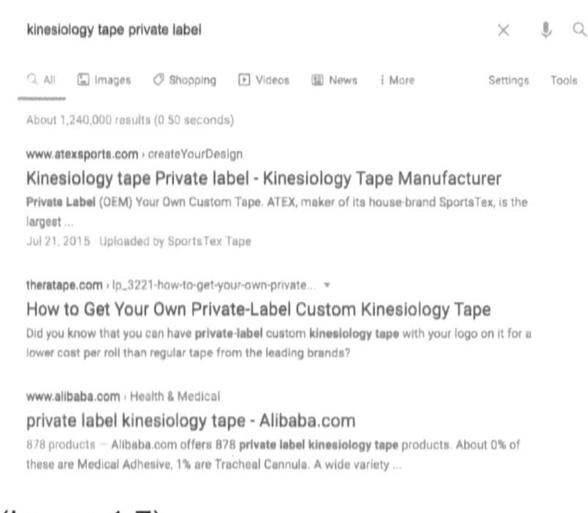

(Image 1.7)

3 – Product Name + Country/State + (manufacturer or private label)

If you want to source locally (assuming you're in the U.S.), then you just have to add the state you want to choose. I recommend that you search for your own state or the state near you first so shipping samples would be easier.

(Image 1.8)

You can also add the word "manufacturer" or "private label" after the state to make your search more specific.

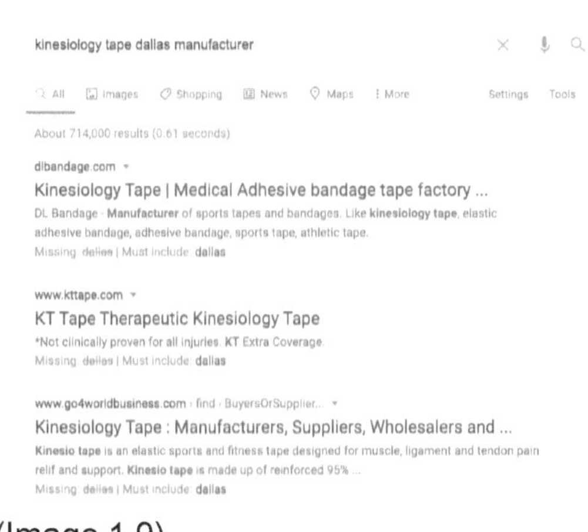

(Image 1.9)

Another thing that you need to consider is the type of product you are selling.

Let's say that you want to sell something that is made from coconut. Try to think about the countries where coconut grows and where this product may be created cheaper.

In this case, the Philippines would be a good choice since they literally have unlimited coconuts there and it is a big source of income and livelihood for the people there.

In this case, your keyword may be your product name + manufacturer + Philippines.

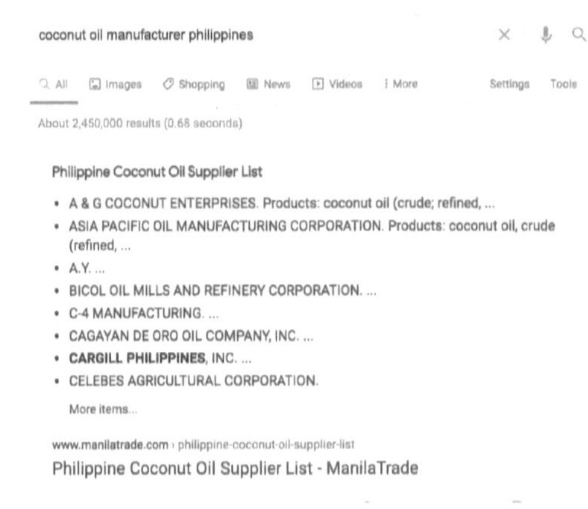

(Image 1.10)

Try to think outside the box and don't limit yourself to just manufacturing in China. There are literally dozens of options out there and you just have to be strategic about your research so you can make the best decision for your business.

4 – Product Name + Manufacturer

This is self-explanatory so I'm not going to spend much time on this. It's as simple as searching for your product name + the word "manufacturer" in it.

BIG TIP: Always Go Through the Top 50 Results from Google

Suppliers aren't always good at marketing themselves, especially with SEO. I recommend that you go through the top 20-50 results because you may find suppliers that aren't really doing SEO but are still awesome with what they do nonetheless.

B – Alibaba

About 70% of the products I sell on Amazon came from Alibaba. I don't particularly think it's because Alibaba is better than other platforms. It's because I was able to build a solid win-win and long-term relationship with the suppliers that I already have.

If you're just getting started, I recommend that you also start with Alibaba. They are the largest aggregator of manufacturers coming from China. 99% of the time, you'll find what you want to sell on Amazon in Alibaba.

For Alibaba, I just start with the keyword related to my product. For example: Yoga Mat

I would also search for Alibaba's suggested keywords as they will add other potential suppliers that offer the same thing.

(Please refer to image 1.11)

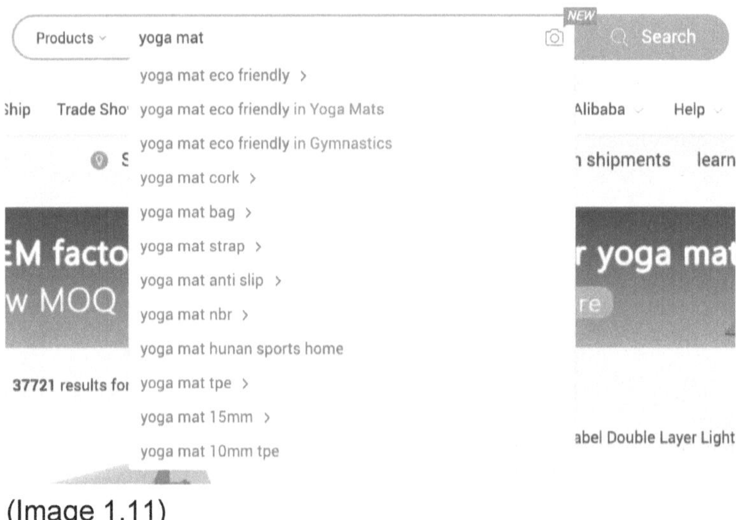

(Image 1.11)

I like to see the following when I'm searching on Alibaba:

1 – Complete Trade assurance, certifications, and verified supplier

(Image 1.12)

2 – They should have more than 4 years experience manufacturing that product.

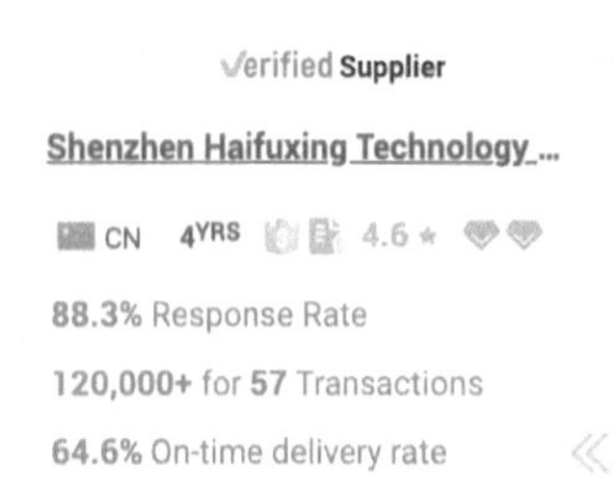

(Image 1.13)

This means they have lots of experience and they are more likely to be easier to work with.

3 - They should have more than 70% response rate

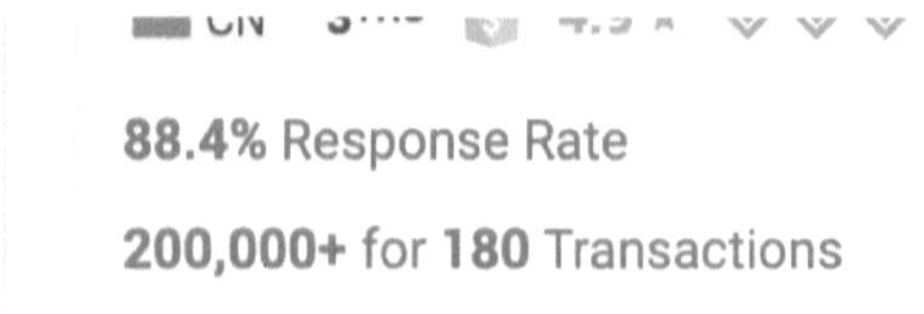

88.4% Response Rate

200,000+ for 180 Transactions

(Image 1.14)

This means they are serious and they are answering people's questions fast.

4 – Complete details

I would like to see a lot of information about their company and about their product. You must take some time to read and understand all of it. I know, it's hard and it takes some time, but it's worth it. All of these are important.

Read their company profile. Look at their website, company history, online reputation, supplier reputation index (this should be at least 2 diamonds) and other relevant information that makes their operation legit.

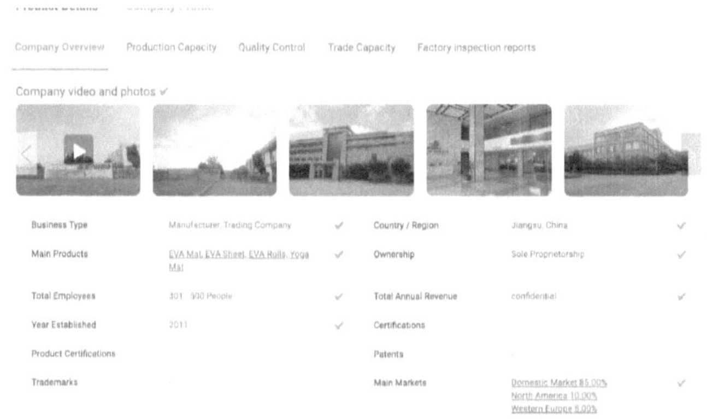

(Image 1.15)

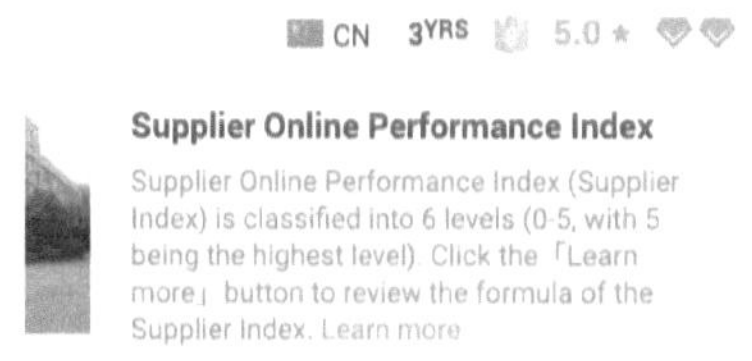

(Image 1.16)

5 - 5x rule

If the manufacturing cost per unit is not at least 4x or 5x the price you can sell it for, then ditch it. For example, if the price per unit of a yoga mat is $5 on Alibaba, then make sure that you can sell it for $25 and above on Amazon.

6 – Delivery Rate

Another crucial information to look at is their delivery rate.

I only work with companies that has at least 80% on-time delivery rate.

200,000+ for **180** Transactions
95.5% On-time delivery rate

(Image 1.17)

Less than that and I'll be very cautious on working with that manufacturer.

CN   **3YRS**   5.0 ★
44.4% On-time delivery rate

(Image 1.18)

C – TTNET.NET

I love this resource because they can give you a lot of different products to choose from and different choices of the product's origin country.

Simply search for your product and you'll find a lot of suppliers ready to talk to you via email/chat/or phone.

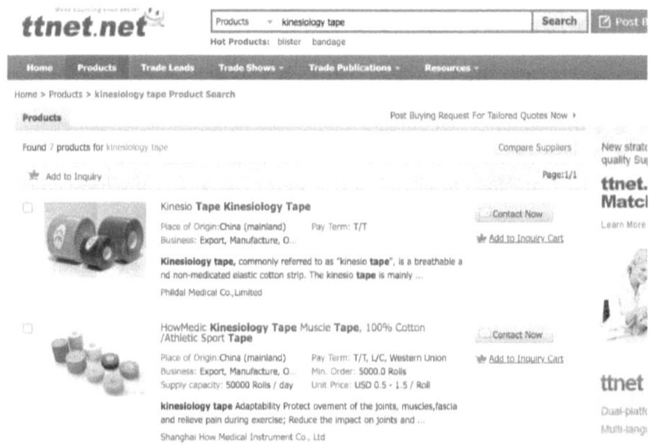

(Image 1.19)

When you are looking for a supplier, make sure that you only deal with the MANUFACTURER and not a trading company.

You can usually find this detail in the product listing but it wouldn't hurt to ask them directly about it. Make it clear that you only want to work with a direct supplier and NOT a trading company.

Product Category:	Adhesive Tapes/n.e.s.
Sales Method:	Export, Manufacture, OEM/ODM
Payment Term:	T/T

(Image 1.20)

AGAIN, ONLY DEAL WITH THE MANUFACTURER.

Wholesalers & Trading companies will add 15-20% to your total Cost of goods sold. Not cool.

In addition, read everything that you can about this company, especially if you plan to do a lot of business with them.

It would also be smart to Google search them and find their websites. Most of these guys in TTNET don't show their website. So you have to do more research.

Also, it would be nice to know their specialty. You only want the best and your customers deserves only the best.

D - HKTDC

Another awesome place to find products is HKTDC.

(Image 1.21)

They have a lot of suppliers from Hongkong, China, and Taiwan.

It's pretty much the same as TTNET, you just have to search for your product and look at different suppliers that may have your product available for production.

When you do your research, make sure that you click on the **Product & Services** option.

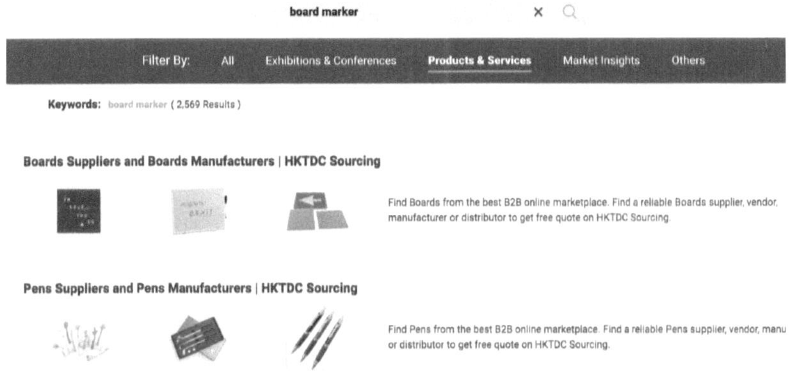

(Image 1.22)

Click on one of the results and then use this criteria for your search.

Tick on "Verified Supplier" for the supplier type.

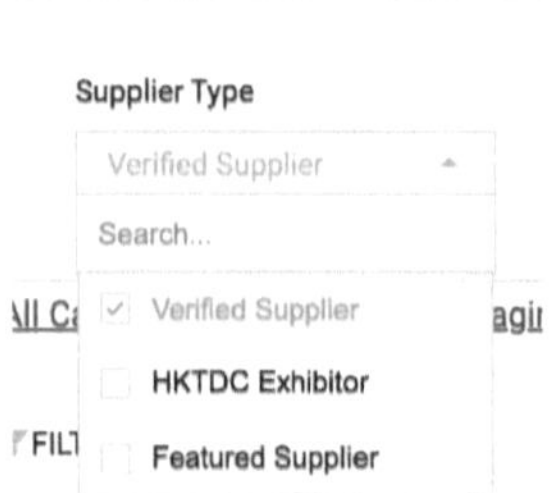

(Image 1.23)

Then choose the country or region that you want to use. I suggest that you just click on all of them, and do the same for factory location.

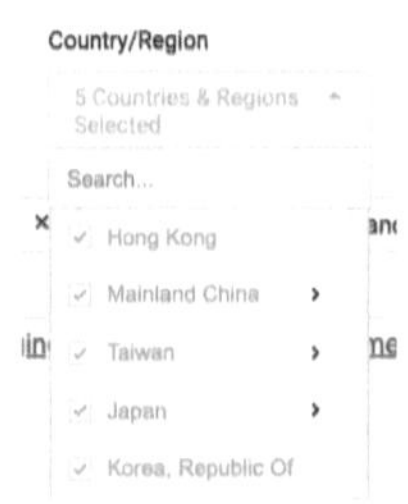

(Image 1.24)

(Image 1.25)

For nature of business, I only tick on "manufacturer" so I get to do business directly with the supplier.

Nature of Business

(Image 1.26)

Choosing any other "nature of business" may lead to higher cost and you want to avoid that especially if you're just getting started.

You may also want to consider only working with manufacturers with GOLD or SILVER verification. This shows that they are a real company with a good reputation.

Within 24 hours

(Image 1.27)

Don't forget to check more details about their business just like what you did with Alibaba and TTNET.

E - Ask Your Social Media Friends

The last option that I recommend is to try and ask your social media friends about potential supplier for the product that you want to sell. Sometimes, a simple post on Facebook or your Instagram story can lead to the best supplier for your product.

It wouldn't really hurt to try and ask publicly. If no one recommends anyone, then just delete your post – no harm done – and move on to using other ways of searching for a supplier.

Chapter 2
Hiring the Best Suppliers

One of the best ways to increase profit margin is to work with the right supplier. You can't just pick anybody that has the best prices. It's a good start but that shouldn't define who you ultimately work with.

For example, I once worked with a supplier from China for a plastic made gym bottle that I used to sell years ago. At first glance, that supplier looks shiny and awesome – they have the best numbers and I'm going to make $3 more profits per item if I went with them. Mind you, I sell around 500 pieces per month at that time so that's an extra $1,500 per month (in addition to the original profit I already calculated) in my pocket that I can use to my bling bling and stuff. The problem was they are a little bit of a pain in the butt to work with. Most of them have a hard time following instruction, some of the people I talked to can hardly understand english, and they tend to reply very late. This could've been an awesome deal but there's so many red flags that I have to weigh-in. At the same time, I also found another Chinese manufacturer that offers it at a higher price and it would only make me an extra $1.5 per piece or an extra $750 per month. However, this seller replies fast, has a better track record, delivers on time and they always message me about stuff related to the product.

Guess who I chose to work with? The second one.

Yes, I made less money but I was also able to have less stress and save more time because of how good they are as a seller and manufacturer. Remember, it's not solely about the profits. It's also about having a good long-term business relationship.

I ended up working with the second manufacturer for the last 4 years and I was also able to save lots of time and money because I already have a reliable company to work with on a long-term basis.

THE PURPOSE OF PRE-RESEARCH

The goal of this chapter is to show you how to do preliminary research so you won't waste your time talking to them for hours and hours only to find out that they are not capable of being your supplier.

We want to make this process seamless and repeatable because you're going to do this over and over again until you find your perfect supplier match.

Here are the 4 preliminary steps you have to do before you hire a supplier and make your first big order.

Step 1 – Find and Save

The first step is to just find suppliers and save their information on a spreadsheet.

I recommend that you create a supplier spreadsheet so you'll be able to track everything that you're doing. By having some kind of spreadsheet, you'll know exactly who you already contacted, what things you said, and other important stuff you need to take note of.

Having a spreadsheet also allows you to see the information in an organized way, which then allows you to make a better decision on who to ultimately work with.

SUPPLIER NAME	CATEGORY	timezone	contact name	email	phone #	skype

I	J	K	L	M	N
moq	leadtime	volume available	date contacted		NOTES?\

(Image 2.1)

For starters, I recommend inputting the following information:

A – Supplier/Manufacturer Company Name

B – Product Name or Product Category

C – Contact Name

D – Contact Email/Skype/Contact Number

E – Minimum Order Quantity They Are Asking For (Note: This is almost always negotiable)

D – Lead Time (This is the number of days or weeks they need to produce the product not including the shipping time)

E – Volume Available (This is the quantity of unit they can produce per month)

F – Date Contact

G – Additional Notes

Do this so you'll never lose track of what's happening with the relationship between you and the supplier.

Step 2 – Making the First Contact, Qualifying, and Getting Price Quotes

I swear, a lot of new sellers treat the first contact as if they're finding hookups on Tinder. They're too casual and they don't command any respect at all.

"Hey, how you doin'?"

"Hi, can you customize this product? How much do I have to pay per piece?"

"Hey, can you sell this product for 200 MOQ instead and lower the price by $1 each?"

The problem with this half-hearted approach is they do not appear professional and they are full of incomplete details necessary to make a buying decision.

From the very first contact, you should have an air of professionalism and they should feel like they are working with a pro.
You want them to feel that they are working with a million-dollar company even if you're only operating in your garage.

Here's an example of the first message I send to manufacturers:

Hi,

My name is Red, a manager and purchasing agent of Ecom X Company LLC.

I am reaching out to inquire about the possibility of working together and creating a long-term business relationship. We are an international e-commerce company based on Los Angeles, California and we are interested in some of the products you offer.

We're looking for a nationwide manufacturer of a product similar to this link:

Amazon.com/productlink
Product dimensions: 2 x 4
Weight: 1lb
Shipping Weight: 1.25lb

Kindly answer the following questions about your product:

#1 – What is the cost of the product per unit including custom packaging (+ our logo) with an order of 500 units, 1,000 units and 2,000 units?

#2 – Can you print our logo in your product?

#3 – Can you provide custom packaging solutions?

#4 – Can you put the UPC in the product?

#5 – Are you able to send a custom sample of the product and how much would you charge if sent via DHL or FedEx to the following address: Your address here

Thank you and I'm looking forward to hearing from you soon,

Red, Lead Product Manager at Ecom X Company

**

This simple message alone can help you separate yourself from other sellers who just message short but unserious-like messages to the manufacturers.

Note: Please don't copy this word for word. However, I do want you to follow the structure of the message.

The key here is to act professional and find out the preliminary details necessary for you to make a better buying decision later.

Another thing to remember: This is not the time to negotiate. That happens a little later in the process when you're ready to make your first big unit order. For now, focus on making sure that the supplier you chose can indeed deliver the product to you the way you want it to.

Step 4 – Requesting Product Samples

Once you already received a reply and you already calculated the numbers (just use the 5X rule) – the next step is to order samples so you can make sure that you have a quality product.

When you order a sample, make sure that it's already what the final product may look like (maybe except for the packaging as this may take time, more money and some back & forth to do). At this point, you just want to know what the actual product would look and feel like when you use it. The packaging itself can later be inspected via HD pictures and videos that your supplier may send you.

Before you order samples, you have to be clear on what you want.

Do you want to add your logo in your product? Where do you want to add it? Are there some type of iterations or differentiations that you want to add to your own private label? You have to know what those things are even before you order a sample.

The sample product will naturally cost you more because you're making them create something with some customization in it. On average, you should expect to pay between $50-$100 for the sample and it should take around 2-4 weeks to get delivered. If you're adding lots of other customization, then it'll be more expensive and you should expect the cost per unit to go up.

Note: I DO NOT recommend that you don't order any sample. Your sample is a crucial part of the process and knowing what kind of product you have can help you decide later on whether to order a large quantity or not.

Chapter 3

Ordering Units, Negotiating for the Best Prices, and the Shipping Process Explained

At this point, you already know the supplier you want to work with. You already have an idea of what your final product would look like, and you are 100% sure that this is the path that you want to take. There shouldn't be any doubt in your mind that this is indeed the product that you want to sell. If so, then you have to go back to product research.

Now it's time to make the order, and more importantly, make the correct order.

Step 1 – Know Thy Units

This is super easy but important nonetheless. First, you have to have an idea of how much you are willing to invest. If Minimum Order Quantity (MOQ) is 500 pieces and it cost $5 per piece, then you better be sure that you have $2,500 to invest – and that's just for the product itself. Remember, you also have to pay for shipping, which is usually around 10%-25% of the total cost of the product itself.

Step 2 – Negotiate MOQ & Price

Here's the mindset that I want you to have when it comes to negotiating the MOQ and/or the price per piece.

NEGOTIATE FOR LONG TERM MUTUALLY BENEFICIAL RELATIONSHIP.

It must be win-win or else, they will harbor ill will even if they ended up working with you.

The first message that you sent (remember that intro message from chapter 2?) will have a big impact on your negotiation. If you appear serious and professional from the onset, then they will respect you. If you appear and sound like a noob, then they will probably pass up on your business.

Now, the price quote that you got from them will usually be the highest price. In fact, they expect you to negotiate.

So how do we actually negotiate a win-win solution?

First, remember that you and the manufacturer have to make a profit for that transaction.

I recommend that you send a counter offer with a price and MOQ that you want to target + your profit computation.

For example, if you want to order 500 pieces of BBQ gloves at $3 each, let them know about your target profit per piece.

Usually, I would put all my expenses for the product including shipping, FBA fees, marketing fees, and every other fee I can think of. Although that wouldn't necessarily be super accurate, I want to let them know that I am only making "this much" profit per piece – and that's the reason why you're negotiating for a better price.

If you show them that after all the expenses, you're only making $2 profit per piece – then they will be more in tuned to negotiate because they know that you're not really making any money from the deal.

At first, you do this strategy and you negotiate based on logic.

Once you already have a good relationship with them, then you can blatantly ask for discounts just because you want to increase your profit margin. Even then, you can always use the same strategy and use numbers for negotiating a better deal.

Now sometimes, the price that they will give you is the best that they can do. Don't try to bargain too hard especially in the beginning. Your goal at this point is to try to move the needle a little.

Again, you have to think WIN-WIN.

If the left-hand wins, then the right hand must win as well.

Step 3 – The Shipping Process Explained

Now I'm going to explain the incredibly misunderstood world of product shipping. A little bit of a warning though, you will not learn everything that there is to know about shipping in this book. The truth is, there will be some things that you just have to learn by actually doing the real thing. However, I'm going to try my best to explain this in a relatively simple, step by step manner.

THE PROCESS:

Once your manufacturer has finished creating the product, did the inspection and it's ready to ship – they will now send the product to their port (for example, from China factory to one of their city's port). From there, it will either be loaded via airplane (air) or a container ship (sea).

From there, it will reach either an airport or a domestic seaport in the U.S.
Once it arrives, U.S. Customs (or whatever country you are in) will inspect the product. Expect this to add a 1-2 weeks delay in the shipping process. The time itself totally depends on a lot of factors like the type of product you are selling and even the season we are currently in. Electronic product usually takes more time to inspect and the Christmas season are usually the busiest months and you should expect your product to have delays during these months (usually November to January).

At this point, all you can do is check your tracking number for updates and the progress of your shipping.

Once the inspection is complete, you can either use a freight forwarder for them to handle the shipping for you or you can send it to your home address or the AMAZON FBA Warehouse itself.

So that is pretty much the entire sequence of shipping from the manufacturer to your doorstep.

Now, allow me to discuss the shipping options and all the minutia of the whole process. Knowing the meaning of shipping terms will absolutely help you clarify the right option for your situation.

Remember, you can mention these to your supplier and if they are a pro, then will understand what these means.

TYPES OF SHIPPING TO USE PART 1: Ex Works, Freight on Board, and Delivery Duty Paid

A - Ex Works or EXW

EXW is when you bear the responsibility of shipping from your supplier's warehouse to their shipping port, to your country's port, and then to your desired address/or the Amazon warehouse. You'll basically do all the work and talk to all the parties that needs to attend to your shipment. Simply put: This is the shipping method for anyone who wants to make their life a living hell.

I absolutely DO NOT recommend using this shipping method unless you hate yourself.

B - Freight on Board or FOB

This is where you share the responsibility of shipping the product with your supplier 50/50. With FOB, your supplier will handle the shipping from their warehouse all the way to your domestic port. From there onwards, you will be 100% responsible for getting it from the port to your address or Amazon's warehouse. Alternatively, you can also hire a freight forwarder to do this for you.

I recommend this method for a little more experienced sellers since it's like the happy middle for saving money and making the items arrived on time.

C - Delivery Duty Paid – DDP

DDP is when the seller is responsible for shipping the product from their warehouse to your doorstep or to Amazon's warehouse. Naturally, this will be more expensive and this may eat out your profits. However, I still recommend that you go for this if the numbers still make sense.

What you have to remember is cheaper isn't always better. Sure, you can save money from doing EXW or FOB – but the fastest way to make money from FBA is to make sure that your products are available for sale in the first place. You cannot make money with a product that isn't there. I know…DUHH… But when you're making these types of decisions, I don't want you to think only about the upfront cost. Think about the opportunity cost as well. The time you spent dealing with shipping could be spent actually marketing the product and having it already LIVE and available for sale on Amazon.

In the beginning, I can understand the hesitation to put more money into the shipping process. Trust me, I do understand the pain of spending more money and having less profit margin for my first product. But you have to think long-term and you have to use this as an opportunity to learn instead.

And that kids, is my long-winded way of saying: Just stick to Delivery Duty Paid (DDP) - or at the very least, FOB.

TYPE OF SHIPPING TO USE PART 2: AIR VS. SEA VS. LAND

The next thing you need to think about is whether you will ship your product by air, by sea, or in some cases, by land.

Truth be told, the best way will almost always be the fastest – which is by air. Almost all types of product can be ship by air unless your product is as big as a car – then in that case, the best option is by sea.

Here are some of the pros of cons of shipping by air, sea, or land.

A - SHIPPING BY AIR

- In most cases, shipping by air is the fastest. Unless there's a customs delay (which rarely happens), then you should expect your product to arrive in between 5-7 days.
- If you use a company like DHL, FedEx, or the UPS then you won't need to use a freight forwarder since these are end-to-end solutions for shipping. If you use UPS, it will typically be at around 7-12 days. Faster shipping allows you to start selling sooner but it may also eat up your profits.
- The one drawback to shipping by air is it is usually the more expensive option.

B - SHIPPING BY SEA

- Shipping by sea is the cheapest option.
- It's awesome for larger shipments.
- But it may take 21-45 days to get delivered, and that's assuming no delay from customs.
- Also, shipping by sea requires you to have a freight forwarder.

C – SHIPPING BY LAND

- This is only available if you're getting your product within the country. Just ask your manufacturer to deliver it to your desired shipping address, and voila – you're in business.
- The shipment may take between 3-14 days to arrive.

How to Save Money

If this is a new product you're selling to the market, then I suggest that you split your shipment by AIR and SEA 50/50.

Shipping by air allows you to start selling sooner which helps you establish a brand and start getting higher rankings on Amazon's search engine. Then shipping the other half by sea allows you to save money thus increasing your profit margins.

If you do this, try to make the order at the same time so the other half of the inventory may arrive by day 30 to day 60.

When Do You Need a Freight Forwarder?

If you chose FOB, then you are going to need a freight forwarder. A forwarder is basically an agent or company that handles the shipping for you once the items arrived at your local air or sea port. They will make the inspections for you and they will basically do all the paperwork and they will send the product to your preferred destination (most of the time, it's on Amazon's warehouse).

Here are some Freight Forwarders to consider:

The Establishment: **FedEx, UPS, DHL**

Forest Shipping – They specialize in FBA, so they are highly recommended. https://forestshipping.com/
OOCL - https://www.oocl.com/eng/Pages/default.aspx
MATSON - http://www.matson.com.cn/

Also, don't be afraid to ask recommendations and questions to your supplier. Most of the time, they are already working with forwarders and then can even give you a discount because you already have a connection.

HOW TO SHIP DIRECTLY TO AN AMAZON FBA WAREHOUSE

This is the path that I recommend you take whether you chose FOB or Delivery Duty Paid.

If you're 100% sure about the quality of your product; you've seen the inspection and you trust your seller with all your hard-earned investment, then it's a good idea to just ship it directly to Amazon's FBA warehouse. It'll add a bit more step in the process but it's well worth the effort and time you'll put into it.

Here's how it works step by step:

Step 1 – Know Your Shipping Option

Step 1 is to know your shipping option. **You can either ship the product to your home or business address or you can ship it directly to Amazon's warehouse.** I highly recommend that you go for the second option. This will make things easier for you. It will also allow you be hands-off when it comes to the shipping process. Now, make sure that the product was inspected properly before you choose this method.

2 – Understand What Labels You Need

To send the shipment directly to Amazon's warehouse, you will need the following:

A – UPC Code. This needs to be in all of your products and it is highly recommended that you use a box design.

B – Carton Label. This is the label that appear at the top of your Master Carton. This is the label that Amazon scans when it arrives in their warehouse.

C – FSNKU. This is an Amazon Specific Label and you need a UPC to get it.

3 – Follow the Amazon Shipping Plan

Step 1 – Go to your Sellers Central account.

Step 2 – Go to Manage Inventory

Step 3 – Choose the product box that you set up for your listing and then click on SEND/REPLENISH INVENTORY.

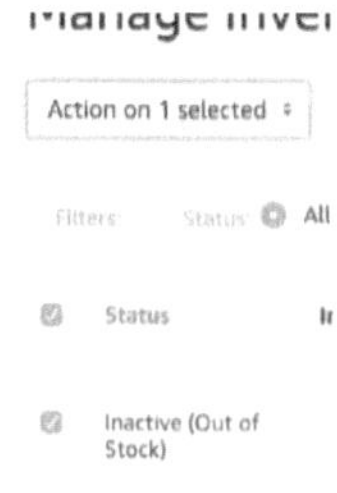

(Image 3.1)

(Image 3.2)

Step 4 – Setup the Ship from Address

Ask your supplier for their full address and input it in the ship from section.

(Image 3.2)

Step 5 – Choose Your Packaging Type

And then choose "case-packed products"

Case-packed products are items that has identical items that has matching SKUs, and each case must have the same number of products. Your supplier should already know how this works so make sure that you ask them about it.

Now, multiple cases can be packed into a larger box called Master Carton, which does not qualify as case-packed and must be split into cases.

Another thing to remember is the word "unit per case" – This refers to the number of items per case and NOT the number of cases per Master Carton.

Okay, this may all sound weird and complicated, but trust me – this will all make sense once you start to actually ship your items and once you start working with your supplier.

Step 6 – Set Quantity

The next step is to set the quantity of your product. Kindly refer to image 3.4 for an example.

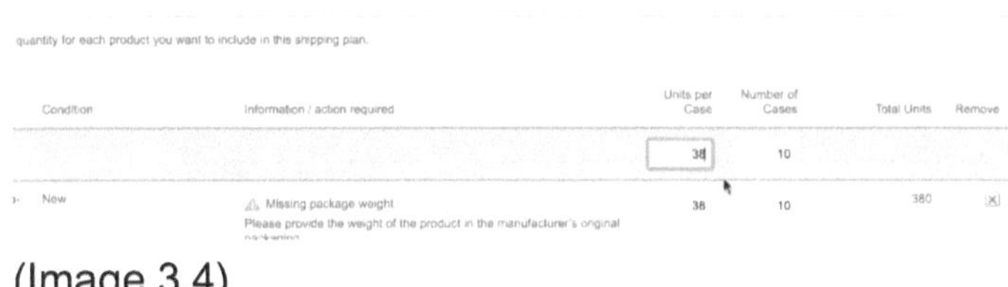

(Image 3.4)

Step 7 – Go to "Prepare Products" section and then click on the show ASIN/FNSKU checkbox. Next, choose "Merchant".

(Image 3.5)

Step 8 – Click on Print labels for this page.

(Image 3.6)

A pdf file will appear and this is the file that you should send to your supplier, to be included in the shipment itself. They will know what to do with this file as long as you clarify that this product goes directly to Amazon.

Step 9 – Review your shipment and choose SMALL
PACKAGE DELIVERY or SPD.

(Image 3.7)

Step 10 – Confirm the details that you input about your
product (weight, numbers of units, etc.)

(Image 3.8)

Step 11 – Print your box labels and then complete the
shipment.

(Image 3.9)

Make sure that you save the box labels that will appear and send that as well to your supplier.

You will get something similar to this: (please refer to image 3.10)

(Image 3.10)

And that's it, you now have completed the process of shipping directly to Amazon's warehouse. Just send all the printed labels to your supplier and they will already know what to do with it.

P.S. If you want a more detailed breakdown on how shipping works, I highly recommend this pdf that was provided by Amazon.

https://images-na.ssl-images-amazon.com/images/G/01/fba-help/QRG/FBA-Shipping-Inventory-to-Amazon.pdf

You can also Google "Amazon FBA shipping guide pdf" if this link didn't work.

Supplier Cheat Sheet – What You Need to Know Before Your First Order

This is the exact cheat sheet that I use for my own business.

You should have the details for all of them before you go through the initial order.

You will get most of the details in the process of talking, researching and negotiating with your supplier.

1 – Name of Supplier

2 – All contact details (email, phone #, skype etc.)

3 – Website

4 – Complete address

5 – Minimum order quantity (MOQ)

6 – What are their packaging and labeling options

7 – Do they do product customization?

8 – Lead time

9 – Shipping Options/methods

10 – Price quotes for MOQ

11- Price quotes for packaging/labeling/customization

12 – The volume of product they can create every month

13 – How does shipping works and what are the fees (from Manufacturer's factory to your warehouse /Amazon FBA - DOOR TO DOOR)

14 – Are there any additional FEES for everything? (shipping, tax, customs)

15 – How does the quality control process works

16 – The exact weight, height and every single specifications of that product

17 – What payment methods will they accept? Warning: Never ever pay via money transfer (Western Union). If they insist, run.

18 – Any possible third party options for shipping, packaging, labeling and product customization?

ADD THE FOLLOWING IF YOU'RE SHIPPING DIRECTLY TO AMAZON FBA'S WAREHOUSE:

19 – Make sure that you print (in pdf) all the labels and send it to your supplier

20 – Always inform your supplier that you are shipping directly to Amazon's warehouse.

I know that all of these may sound a lot.

But if you come to think of it, 30% of the list can be answered through your own research. The other 70% can be answered in just two 15 minute phone calls!

Also, if you really wanted to stand out in this business, talk to them via phone/skype and they will take you more seriously. When it comes to talking with suppliers, email is overrated! (Unless it's the first contact).

You'll probably be uncomfortable talking to them in the beginning, but that's alright. Would you rather be comfortable and broke? Or would you rather be uncomfortable at the beginning and eventually rich?

You decide.

P.S. While you're waiting for your product to arrive, don't mess around and just do nothing. Set up your listing sales pages, go research your keywords, and go market your potential products to future buyers.

Chapter 4

Barcodes and FBA Fees Demystified

In this chapter, I'm going to explain what barcodes are and how each type differs. I know that there's a lot of confusion when it comes to terms like UPC, FNSKU, GS1 and all of these seemingly random letters and numbers and how it relates to your Amazon business.

Let's start with the most common one:

UPC: Universal Product Code – A 12-digit barcode unique to each product.

Everything that you buy online and offline will have its own UPC unique to each product. (This is especially true in 1st world countries).

Remember the thing that the grocery store scanned when you bought your 2nd jar of peanut butter this week? That's a UPC. It's basically a tracker and a source of information for the product. Every product should have that – at least, every legal one. Different products will always have a different UPC – unless it's an illegal operation, then no two products will have the same UPC.

GS1 – Global Standards – Is the BEST and most legitimate place to buy UPC barcodes.

I used to recommend other ways to get UPC but I know better now and this is the only way that you should get one today.
Don't forget that Amazon will verify the legitimacy of your UPC by checking GS1's database. If your UPC didn't match GS1's database, then Amazon will consider it as invalid.

There are 2 ways to buy GS1's UPC.

The first one is to get it directly from GS1 via their website:

https://www.gs1.org/standards/get-barcodes

It cost $250 per 10 UPC and + $50 annual fee to register to your name or your company name.

You can also use a third party like Nationwide Barcode at a much cheaper rate at only $12 each.

https://www.nationwidebarcode.com/purchase-barcodes/barcodes-for-amazon/

It will also be cheaper if you get it by bulk. Here's the current pricing table as shown in their website.

GS1 Originated UPCs/EANs – Volume Pricing

UPC/EAN Quantity	Your Price	Total
1	$12.00	$12.00
5	$7.50	$37.50
10	$4.25	$42.50
25	$2.25	$56.25
50	$1.28	$64.00
100	$0.80	$80.00
250	$0.60	$150.00
500	$0.40	$200.00
1,000	$0.30	$300.00
2,500	$0.20	$500.00
5,000	$0.16	$800.00
10,000	$0.14	$1400.00

(Image 4.1)

They also run promos every now and then which allows you to save between 10%-40% on UPC.

Note: Do not buy from resellers on eBay, Fiverr or any other websites outside GS1 and Nationwide Barcode.

FNSKU: Fulfillment Network Stock Keeping Unit – This is Amazon's own barcode.

FNSKUs are used to track every product that goes in and out of Amazon's warehouse. These should be in every unit that you are selling.

Note: The UPC you purchased can be used to generate unique FNSKU from Amazon. Now, it is possible to use just a UPC but I highly recommend that you also generate FNSKU so Amazon will have an easier time locating and managing your product.

***

Here's how all these barcodes tied up together:

1 – You need a UPC so you can create your listing.
2 – Only purchase UPC from reliable suppliers like GS1 or Nationwide Barcode.
3 – You are allowed to only have UPC without the FNSKU but it's better to have FNSKU so Amazon can track your product better.
4 – You can generate your free FNSKU in Seller Central when you create your product listing.

I recommend reading this short blog post for more information about FNSKU.

https://www.shipcalm.com/blog/fnsku/

FBA FEES EXPLAINED:

Now let's talk about how to calculate all the FBA fees that you need to pay when you sell through Amazon FBA. You will add these to your expense column and you should also take this into account as you compute your profit per product unit sold.

The first fee to consider is the selling fee. To sell on Amazon as an individual, you can start for $0 but it's only limited to 40 items per month plus there's a $0.99 fee for every unit sold + the shipping cost. To sell on Amazon as a professional, you need to pay a monthly fee of $39.99 per month. On top of this monthly fee, these are the other ones that you have to pay if you chose to have them manage your inventory and ship the product for you.

Please refer to image 4.2 and 4.3 for reference.

#1 - Fulfillment (Shipping) Fee:

Size tier	Max dimension	Shipping weight [1]	Packaging	Fulfillment fee per unit [2]
FBA Small and Light	16" x 9" x 4"	4 oz. or less	0.7 oz.	$1.97
		4+ oz. to < 10 oz.	0.7 oz.	$2.39
Small standard	15" x 12" x 0.75"	10 oz. or less	4 oz.	$2.50
		10+ to 16 oz.	4 oz.	$2.63
Large standard	18" x 14" x 8"	10 oz. or less	4 oz.	$3.31
		10+ to 16 oz.	4 oz.	$3.48

(Image 4.2)

Depending on the weight and dimension of the product, the cost will vary from $1.97 up to an average of $5 per unit. It can go up to 100s of dollars but that's only applicable for very heavy and huge shipments.

#2 - FBA Storage Fee:

FBA storage fees *

Inventory storage fees are charged monthly based on the daily average volume (measured in cubic feet) for the space your inventory occupies in Amazon fulfillment centers. The volume measurement is based on unit size when properly packaged and ready to ship.

Month	Standard size	Oversize
January - September	$0.75 per cubic foot	$0.48 per cubic foot
October - December	$2.40 per cubic foot	$1.20 per cubic foot

(Image 4.3)

The storage fee will also depend on the dimension of your product and the month of the year as October to December are usually very busy and full-packed months for ecommerce. Expect to pay $0.75 per cubic foot of storage from January to September and $2.40 per cubic foot storage during the Holiday season.

There are some other fees that may occur depending on your product but these ones are the basic fees that you will always have to pay for if you're using FBA.

To learn more about fees, I recommend that you check out this link:

https://sell.amazon.com/pricing.html

Chapter 5

Supplier Related Practices

of the Most Profitable

Ecommerce Business Owners

By now, you already have a process of researching, evaluating, and hiring a supplier from start to finish. In this chapter, I want to give you some of the best tips that I can give when it comes to working with suppliers. All of these tips may seem generic or even common advice, but trust me, these little tips can help you a lot as you navigate the sometimes complicated (but still awesome) world of Amazon FBA.

Tip #1 – Build Long Term Win-Win Relationships

Always choose long-term over short-term wins. This may cost you a buck or two of profit in the beginning but you have to believe in win-win relationships. The manufacturer has to make their target profit per product as well. Don't worry because as you build the relationship, you'll be able to ask for more discounts and you'll be able to negotiate better prices. Most manufacturers want you to stay with them for as long as possible. They understand that getting new customers is much harder than retaining one. If they are a good supplier, they will offer you the best price that they can offer – as simple as that.

Tip #2 – Calculate the Profits Conservatively + Proper Cost Evaluation

When you're doing the pre-research for the product and the supplier, be conservative with your calculations. Following the 5X rule is a safe bet for you to hit breakeven. If the product per unit cost is $3, then you have to be able to sell it for at least $15 on Amazon to hit breakeven or to profit. Remember that you'll also have other expenses like shipping cost, FBA fees, FBA storage fees, UPC, etc.

Tip #3 – Contact as Many Suppliers as Possible

It's very unlikely that you'll find your main supplier just by messaging the first supplier listing you'll see on Alibaba. The truth is, it may take tens if not hundreds of messages before you truly find that one or two suppliers that you will eventually work with for your future products. But once you found that one supplier, it'll be so worth it because they can save you lots of time, money, and even effort in making the manufacturing and shipping as seamless as possible.

I highly recommend that you message as many suppliers as you can. I know that you're tempted to just message 3 and choose the one that replies, but you have to be patient and stick to the criteria and standard that we set for ourselves. Just be patient and follow the process I laid out in this book.

Tip #4 – Clear Instructions + Confirm Things Before the Order

Always give them clear instructions whenever you are passing some kind of details about your product or shipment. If you want them to put a label on your package, then be clear and let them know exactly where to put it. Or if you don't know where to put it, ask them questions about past customers and how they did it for their own FBA shipments.

Also, make sure that you confirm details before you finalize your order. Follow the cheat sheet I gave you in chapter 3.

Tip #5 – Choose Quality Over Price

In the beginning, you will be tempted to choose price over quality. I understand what you're going through. You're nervous about not making any profit and losing your hard-earned investment. But you have to think about the customers here. If your customers are happy, then they will leave 5-star reviews and you will be able to charge a little more for your product because of the quality as well. Choosing to earn a few dollars of profit in the beginning probably means making thousands later.

Tip #6 – Address Supplier Concerns Respectfully

If you're having issues with your suppler (and trust me you will), then ask them about it respectfully. Being rude and condescending will only lead to a sour business relationship. Always be clear on where you stand, and let them know that you appreciate the work they are putting in. Then address your concern and let them know that you want X thing to be solved by a certain target date.

Tip #7 – Pay on Time

Manufacturers adore customers who always pay on time. If you say that you're going to pay 50% before x date, then pay it at least 2-3 days before that set-date.

Tip #8 – Pick the Right Shipping Method

Air shipping, although faster, isn't always better in all cases. Sometimes, shipping by sea may fit your product better (this is especially true for heavy and/or huge items). Another thing to consider is your current financial situation. Hey, if you can't afford shipping by air then by all means, go for sea shipping for now and sacrifice a little bit of time before you can sell your product on Amazon. In the beginning, you probably have more time than money anyway so there's no point in losing sleep about this.

Tip #9 – Put Everything into a Contract

I am not a lawyer and I cannot give legal advice but make sure that you put everything into a contract so you won't get taken advantage of by the supplier. The most important ones are the quality of the product and what it should look like, the price, the manufacturing lead time, and the method of shipping to be used for the package.

Conclusion

THE TRUTH ABOUT THE AMAZON FBA BUSINESS

I wish I could tell you that finding an A+ supplier is easy. I wish I could tell you that you could just pick any supplier and then you'll never have to worry about doing anything at all. But it doesn't work that way. There's a lot of tasks to be done and many people will quit along the way. You have to persevere, go through some growing pains, and learn every step of the way.

Here's a recap of the process:

Step 1 – Learn to find where the best suppliers are.

Step 2 – Hire the Best Suppliers by making the right evaluation.

Step 3 – Make the correct order, negotiate the best prices and choose the right shipping option.

Step 4 – Identify the right barcodes you need for your business and learn to calculate your FBA fees.

Step 5 – Wrap it up with the right foundation by following the best practices I recommended in chapter 5.

***

Right now, I understand that there's also a lot of temptation to just buy another Amazon FBA coaching program from tons of gurus out there. But the truth is you probably won't learn something from them that you won't already learn just by spending a few bucks buying the best-selling books on Amazon about FBA. Start with that because it's cheaper and you'll probably save more time and money since it only takes a few hours to read a book while watching a monstrous 40 hours online course will take a huge chunk of your time. I would rather have you spend that time taking action and making things happen for your business. I wish you all the best in this journey.

Talk soon,

Red

Review Request

As you might already know, reviews are the lifeblood of every author out there. If you found some value in this one, allow me to humbly ask for a review on Amazon as it does help in spreading my message.

Thank you, and good luck on your e-commerce business.

Fulfillment by Amazon for Beginners

If you like to learn a simple and step by step way of getting started with Amazon FBA, I recommend that you check out my other books AMAZON FBA Step by Step (by Red Mikhail), FBA Product Research 101 and Amazon Keyword Research 101 as well.

These are also available as audiobooks.

Just like this one, these 3 has a very simple language and conversational tone to it. If you found this book valuable, then you will like those 3 books as well.

OTHER BOOKS

I also have other books about making money online through different ways, check them out here:

Amazon's Associate Program
One Hour Dropshipping System
Amazon Product Listing Formula

AMAZON FBA FUTURE UPDATES:

We're just scratching the surface. In the next few months, I'm going to launch a series of books about:

FBA Advance Traffic & Marketing Strategies

Amazon Wholesaling

Amazon Retail Arbitrage

Amazon Dropshipping

And many more books related to Amazon FBA.

If you want to make sure that you get a notification when these books go LIVE, just simply follow my Amazon author page here:

https://www.amazon.com/Red-Mikhail/e/B00X3KJ2TO/

(Click the follow button on that page to get instant updates from Amazon)

Amazon FBA Sales Boost

33 Little Tricks to Increase Your Amazon Private Label Sales, Get Organic Free Traffic, and Create a More Profitable FBA Ecommerce Business

[Amazon FBA Business Series – Part 5]

Red Mikhail

TABLE OF CONTENTS

Title, Keywords, Description, Features, Seller Feedback, Brand Registry, the Buy Box, Product Classification, etc.

Value Skewing, Product Inserts, Product Differentiation, Purchase Add-Ons, Variety, Product Options, etc.

Amazon PPC, Facebook Ads, Instagram Influencers, Reviewers Program, Lightning Deals, etc.

Introduction

Welcome to part 5 of the Fulfillment by Amazon business series. In this book, I am going to show you 33 different ways to boost your FBA sales. If you're not familiar with this type of business yet, then I highly recommend that you read at least part 1 and part 2 of the series' first. Those 2 books (Amazon FBA step by step and FBA Product Research 101) will give you a great foundation on how you can get started with Amazon FBA.

Just like my other books, you should expect a straight to the point, no B.S. kind of guide. I won't bore you with useless details and I definitely don't need to tell you my life story. If you've been reading my books for a while now, then you already know that I go straight to the actionable and important stuff.

If you're the type of person who hates fluff, then this book is for you.

Overview

When most people think about AMAZON SALES, they only think about the marketing part. They think about product promotions and advertising. The truth is, marketing is only a third of the process. When it comes to Amazon ecommerce sales, you have to think about the following:

Optimization, Product, and Marketing.

Optimization is about maximizing the tools that you have at your disposal. These are things like product titles, keyword research, pricing, product category, etc.

Think of optimization as your most low effort foundational work that will have a surprisingly big impact on your sales. If you don't believe what I'm saying then try it out for yourself. Create 2 similar listings: One applying the lessons from this book and the other ignoring the strategies that I will show you. I guarantee you that the first listing will do at least 2x better when it comes to sales.

Product is about making sure that your customers have options so they can have the best buying experience. This is all about giving them various choices like colors, sizes, quality of materials, etc. This part discusses the concept of "value skewing" and how it can help you dominate your market by having a superior product.

Marketing is about using the right medium to promote your products. Mediums like Amazon PPC, Facebook Ads, Instagram Marketing, Lightning Deals, Amazon's Reviewer Program, etc. This is what people usually think about when it comes to increasing sales. But as you already know, this is only 1/3 of the whole pie. I bet that you'll easily increase your sales by at least 50% even if you only applied part 1 and part 2 of this training. In part 3, I'll show you the best practices to follow so you can maximize these promotion platforms and increase your sales even more.

Some of the ideas are easy to implement and then there are some that will take more time and effort to do. One idea may not get you the amount of sales you are aiming for, but when combined, can boost your sales up to more than 100% of what you currently have right now.

I don't necessarily think that you have to apply each and every one of the ideas. However, I do hope that you'll implement at least 20% of what you'll read. I promise you, doing that alone will do wonders to your FBA business.

Here's my best recommendation for you. Suspend your disbelief for a moment, read every single page of this book, and then choose something that resonates with you.

I'm super excited that you're here, let's get started, shall we?

Part 1

Optimization Ideas

Sales Boost Idea #1 - Optimize Your Title

I will tell you straight up that your title is the most important text in your listing. It could literally be the difference between $100 months and $1,000 months. Why? Because your title tells Amazon and the customers what your product is. Remember, since Amazon is a search engine for products, the customers are looking for the exact product that will either:

A – Solve their problem

B – Fulfill their needs or wants

If your title doesn't fully indicate that it is the product that the customers need, then there's no way they would even click at your listing.

Another important thing to remember about title is that it is heavily weighted for keyword rankings. I have no idea what the exact percentage is (only Amazon knows that). But I do know that your title plays a major role when it comes to Amazon SEO and keyword rankings.

Here are some guidelines to take note of when it comes to product titles:

1 – It must not exceed 200 characters including spaces. Treat these 200 characters as if they are prime real estate and maximize their use.

2 – Do not use any promotional text like: free, sale, discounted, buy now, etc.

3 – Do not use any subjective terms like: best, fastest, most affordable, cheapest, etc. These are words that are harder to define and Amazon does frown upon sellers who uses subjective terms.

4 – Do state the quantity of the product. For example: 1 gallon, 1 liter, 5 pieces, 2 packs, etc.

5 – Do not use any special characters like: "" or *.

6 – Most importantly, do not stuff them with unrelated keywords. If your product is a guitar cord, then do not put any keyword that is unrelated to a guitar cord. I shouldn't have to say this but I see beginner sellers do this just for the sake of adding keywords. Amazon hates it when you do this. It messes up their algorithm and it gives the customers a terrible buying experience. Imagine looking for a bread maker and seeing lots of random "dog breeding" books instead. Yikes!

Here's the title formula that I recommend you follow:

Title formula: Brand Name + Primary Keyword/Product Name + Main Features (Quantity, Benefits, Uses)

Examples:

Bambino *Bamboo Toothbrush, BPA Free Soft Bristles, Eco Friendly, Compostable Toothbrushes, 10 Pieces.*

__Greener Chef__ Extra Large Bamboo Cutting Board for Kitchen, Organic Wood Butcher Block – Wooden Carving Board for Meat and Vegetables - 18 x 12.5

Make sure that you put your most important keywords in your title. These should be keywords that are getting the majority of searches according to your research.

Sales Boost Idea #2 - Target the Right Keywords for Amazon SEO

The keywords that you will use will pretty much determine whether you'll make money on Amazon or not. Why? Because Amazon is a search engine. People are looking for products directly instead of trying to find more information about something (books are the exception).

You will use these keywords for your title, description, features, Amazon keyword optimization (when you create your listing), etc.

Here's how you create a keyword list:

Step 1 - Create Master Spreadsheet. Use this file as the storage for all your keywords.

Step 2 - Use Amazon.com to search for competitors. Search for your product on Amazon and look at the top 10 results. Copy and paste the relevant keywords that you'll find.

Example:

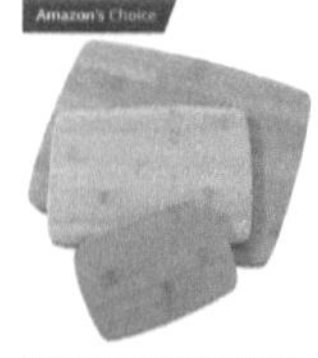

[Image 1.1]

In this example [refer to image 1.1], the keywords that I found are:

Organic Bamboo Cutting Board
Cutting Boards
Carving Board
Chopping Board for Meat and Vegetable

Continue adding keywords to your spreadsheet until you have at least 100. Most of the time, you will find terms that'll appear over and over again. That's where we utilize a tool called Helium10.

Step 3 - Use Helium10 to rearrange keywords. Helium10 is a free tool that you can use to rearrange your keywords. You can use this to cut the fat and remove the keywords that appears over and over again. Remember, if you have keywords like: "Bamboo toothbrush" and "Bamboo toothbrushes", Amazon will automatically count the word "bamboo" as only one keyword so there's no need to repeat mentioning that keyword again and again.

Original keywords

Total characters: 11827 Total words: 1645

bamboo toothbrush
toothbrush
best toothbrush
charcoal toothbrush
kids electric toothbrush
baby toothbrush
biodegradable toothbrush
wooden toothbrush
eco toothbrush
eco friendly toothbrush
gum toothbrush

Output settings

Add only spaces   Remove duplicates
One word/phrase per line   Maintain phrases
Add commas no space   Protect numbers
Add commas with space   Convert to lowercase
Include word frequency count   Remove common words
                                   Remove single words
                                   Remove single letters

[Image 1.2]

Use the following output setting:

1 – One word/phrase per line
2 – Remove duplicates
3 – Convert to lower case

Then on the right side of the original keyword section, click on **frequency**.

When you look at your keywords, you will see the most frequent keywords that are searched over and over again.

Most likely, the first 5-10 results are your main keywords. They are the keywords where more than 40% of your traffic will come from if you're on the first page of Amazon for those keywords.

[Image 1.3]

The next step is to browse your list and look for non-relevant keywords that you can remove.

Remove the keywords that has nothing to do with your product.

Once you're done with that step, just click the "Add Only Spaces" in the output settings to re-arrange your keywords.

The results are your main keywords that you can use for your titles, description, features, etc.

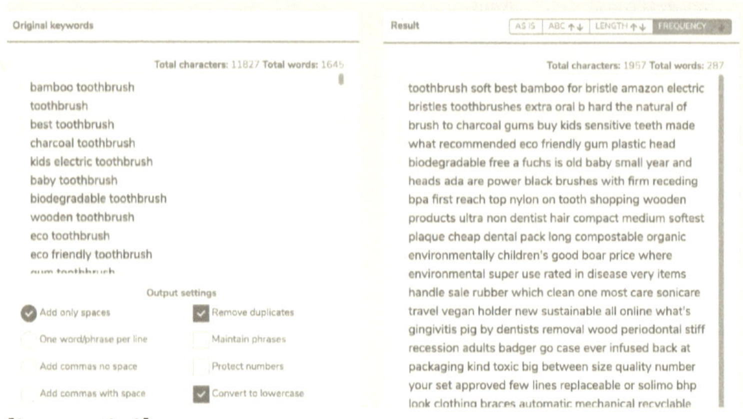

[Image 1.4]

The final step is to click save which lets you download the list as a text file.

If you want to find out more and go in depth on keyword research (without spending any money on tools), I recommend that you check out my book Amazon Keyword Research.

https://www.amazon.com/gp/product/B08JHGWPVF

Sales Boost Idea #3 – Optimize Your Product Images

You already know how important a product image is. You probably won't buy something that looks like the photos were taken from the 50s. Instead of blabbing on how you should get professional photos (which you should be doing), let me talk about the technical aspect of Amazon product images instead.

1 – Image Priority

As of the writing of this book, Amazon allows up to 9 images for your product. Make sure that you maximize the number of allowed photos you can upload on your listing. Try different angles so the customers can look at your product with different point of views, literally speaking.

Also, assign priority to each image – that means that first 3 images that they should see are the best ones. For example, if you are selling a lawn mower – then they should see the product as a whole for the first 3 photos. Next, you can add pictures while the product is in action. See image 1.5, 1.6 and 1.7 for examples.

[Image 1.5]

[Image 1.6]

2 – Technical Image Requirements

A – Image Size: It should be at least 1,000 pixels in width or height.

B – Background Color: Only use white background when you're featuring a product.

C – File Format: Upload using JPEG, PNG, GIF or TIFF.

D – Color Mode: sRGB and CMYK are acceptable.

E – Image Frame: Your product should fill 80%-85% of the frame.

3 – Amazon-Based Standard

Only use actual photos of the product. Vectors, illustrations, drawing, graphics, and text overlays will make your listing look unprofessional.

4 – Use Variety

Try to be creative when it comes to your product images. Use different angles, show the product in action, show the packaging, add key information, and make your product as exciting as possible.

This is where a professional product photographer can help you big-time! Check out their past works before you hire somebody and make sure that they are taking professional, clean, and high-quality images.

5 – Add Key Information

For most products, you can feature some kind of key information that will make your product standout. It can be a material that you use or a key feature that makes your product one of a kind.

For example, if your bamboo toothbrush has BPA free nylon bristles and biodegradable handle, then you can also feature that on your product photos. This gives your customers more information about the item and it highlights what is so special about your product.

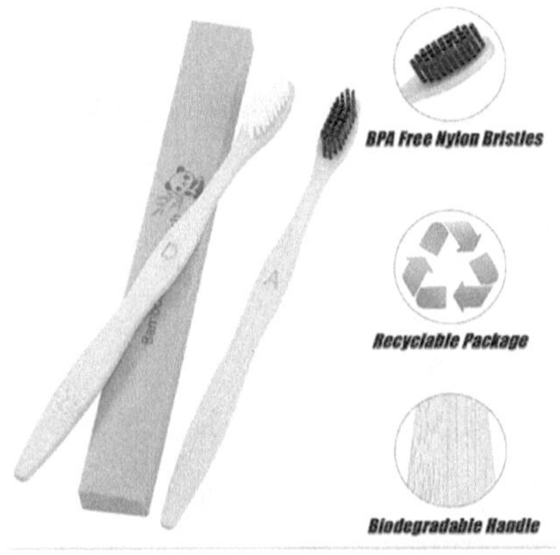

[Image 1.7]

Sales Boost Idea #4 - Improve Your Product Description

First of all, let me define what the product description IS NOT.

Product description is not the text that you see beside the product images. Those are bullet points. Product descriptions are also not the place where you duplicate and copy what you already said in the bullet points.

So, what does a product description do?

A good product description gives the **features** of the product. In my opinion, it should be short and no more than 7 lines for the features and no more than 4 lines for the technical aspects of the product.

So instead of doing a long-winded paragraph about your product:

These durable and biodegradable **toothbrushes have ergonomically designed handles made from Moso bamboo and powered by medium and BPA Free Nylon bristles.** So, our toothbrushes are perfect for those who care about the environment and pursue a zero waste lifestyle.

We are closer to our goal of making the Earth an eco-friendly and cruelty-free place. Moso Bamboo is one of the most sustainable resources on Earth and native to China and Taiwan. It can grow in damaged and nutrients depleted soil and due to its rapid regrowth cycle it can be harvested with virtually no environmental impact. Moso Bamboo is not eaten by Giant Pandas, which is also a good news for all panda lovers.

[Image 1.8]

You should instead do something like this: [refer to image 1.9]

☑ Has medium nylon bristles. Strong enough to offer plenty of polishing power, but gentle enough to not to cause enamel damage.

☑ Dries fast and does not absorb water. Last long as plastic toothbrushes.

☑ Comes in a recyclable box. A perfect gift for a housewarming or any eco-minded friend.

☑ Pack of 4 toothbrushes. Great for a small to medium sized family.

☑ Non-Charcoal Toothbrush

[Image 1.9]

It should be in bullet form. It should be easy & fast to read, and it should give them additional reasons to choose your product over the competition.

You can also add dimension and specs, key information they need to know, plus any warranty or guarantee that your company provides (if there's any).

Check out this example below: [refer to image 1.9]

Product description

Color: Black

This 1500W Mini Ceramic Heater from Joy Pebble utilizes industry leading ceramic heating discs for ultra-warm heat transfer in small spaces. Ceramic heating is the latest technology in mini space heaters and provides a faster, safer and more energy efficient method of heating than traditional space heaters. At the flick of switch, the ceramic fan heater will produce a stream of warm air to quickly and effectively heat the area in front of the heater.

Product description:
Product weight: 3.6 lbs
Noise: 30-40db
Color: black and white
Material: ABS plastic
Power unit: AC power supply
Volt: 110v
Watts: 750 / 1500W
Special properties: dump power off, overheat protection, adjustable power
Included: hot air blower space heater, instruction manual
Product Dimensions: W8.9"*D6.1"*H9.4"

[Image 1.9]

For the main description, I would actually change that to a bullet point style instead of having 4-5 sentences in one paragraph. Also, take note of the "special properties or special instructions" part as you may need to let your customers know about that as well depending on the type of product that you have.

Sales Boost Idea #5 - Use Punchy Features & Bullet Points

After your title, your bullet points are the most important part of your listing. Those bullet points should be short and punchy. Meaning: They have to show the advantages of choosing your product over the other products on Amazon. In addition, they must not be bored with technical details that doesn't relate to what they really want or need. For example, if you're selling a bamboo toothbrush, then you're most likely dealing with a customer who wants to protect the earth in her own little way. In this case, you have to show her the features that actually matches her goals. You can mention that your product is BPA FREE, biodegradable, and eco-friendly.

Here's the formula that I follow when it comes to product features:

Line #1 - Feature + Benefits

The first line should give them the #1 most important benefit of the product.

Line #2 - Feature + Benefits

The 2nd line shows them the 2nd biggest benefit and feature of the product.

Line #3 – Differentiate

The next line should give them some kind of reason why your product is different from the others. This usually comes from having a product that is actually better than your competitors (I know, new concept right? Lol). You cannot fake this one, so make sure that you have a good product.

Line #4 - Twist the Knife + Solve the Problem

In the 4th line, I explain to them what problem this product solves and then I give them the solution for it.

For example, you can say that your product is 100% biodegradable which helps the earth so they don't have to worry about polluting the environment anymore.

Line #5 - Guarantees

I give them a guarantee that the product works or else they can send it back to me and get a 100% refund (mention this if you do offer some).

***

In order to follow this formula, you have to know who your customer is. You have to know their main motivation for buying a product like yours. You can usually do this research by reading the positive and negative reviews of your competitors.

If you want a shortcut on writing your bullet points, you can just read the bullet points of your most reviewed competitors and just rephrase their bullets. Look at the main points they are targeting and use them for your bullets as well.

Sales Boost Idea #6 - Add a Video to Your Amazon Listing

A note before we start. This idea is only open for owners who are already approved for the Amazon Brand Registry Program which we will discuss later.

A lot of sellers won't bother doing a video for their product because it does take some additional work on their part. Now, you don't have to do this when you launch your product but it does help in converting more customers. I recommend that you launch without it but then immediately work your butt off so you can add it on your listing as soon as possible.

Videos are great because they can show the product in flesh. You can show that a real human being is actually using the product. They also have higher retention rates and customers are more likely to buy if they are engaged through your video. Another benefit of videos is they are great for SEO. They can add a lot of traffic to your listing and you don't even have to pay for it.

Here's a few things to remember when you're doing a video for your product listing:

A – The video should show the product's features and benefits. Think of it as the video version of your bullet points.

B – When it comes to video, lighting and audio is key. Make sure that you hire a professional to shoot the video for you. You don't have to spend thousands of dollars to do this. A simple 30-second video of your product + text overlay (which mentions the features) will do.

Here's an example that you can copy:

https://www.youtube.com/watch?v=BMKjRC9r2zk&
C – Adding customer video reviews can also be a substitute.

D – You can upload your video through Amazon's Enhance Brand Content feature.

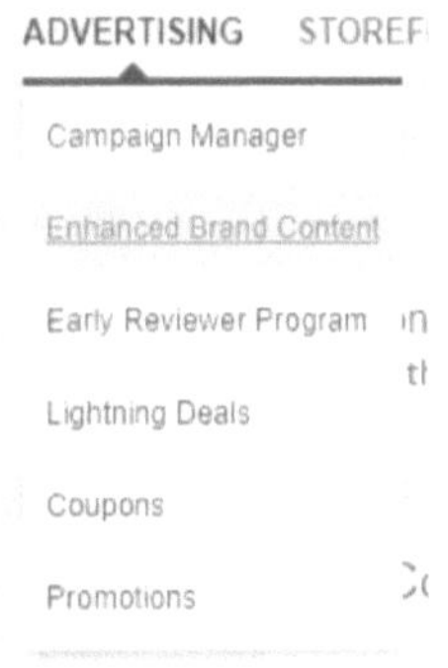

[Image 1.10]

Just follow these steps:

1 – Enter the SKU representing the ASIN of the product you want to use for EBC.

2 – Select your preferred template and fill the text and image slots.

3 – Follow the onscreen prompts and upload the following:

Video file, Image thumbnail, video title, and video description.

4 – Save the changes and submit the content for validation and approval.

Source of instruction:
https://www.sellerapp.com/help/article/add-video-amazon-listing/

Sales Boost Idea #7 - Remove Negative Seller Feedback (Review Section and Feedback Profile)

Negative feedback sucks.

It can affect your sales and how potential customers perceived your product's value. Not every negative feedback can be removed but we must try to erase them whenever possible.

So when can we request for Amazon to remove a negative feedback?

Case #1 – When customers used "obscene language" and "personally identifiable information".

You can request for that feedback to be removed if it contains R-rated language like in a movie. Would you want your kid to read this review? Would it be perfectly okay for them to see the language that was used? If not, then you can contest that feedback. In addition, you can also request to remove a review if there are some personal details that may affect you or the customer.

Case #2 – If the review has nothing to do with the product itself.

If the reviews on the product page and/or your seller profile has nothing to do with the product itself, then you can also request for it to be removed. For example, if an order is late or there has been some issues with fulfillment, then Amazon will take responsibility for that issue and will include a comment that says something like this:

"This item was fulfilled by Amazon, and we take responsibility for this fulfilment experience."

Here's how to remove negative feedback:

Option 1 – Contact Amazon

Open your seller central account and go to

Select Account Settings > Orders > Customer feedback problems.

Send a short message explaining why you think the feedback should be removed in the first place.

Here's an example message:

Hi, I've received a feedback from Alex K. on [order number] and it looks like the comment was based on unsatisfactory customer experience. Is there any way we can remove this feedback on my profile?

Here is the comment:

[Insert feedback here]

Thank you,

Red

You will receive a message that looks like this if you're successful in removing that feedback. [Refer to Image 1.11]

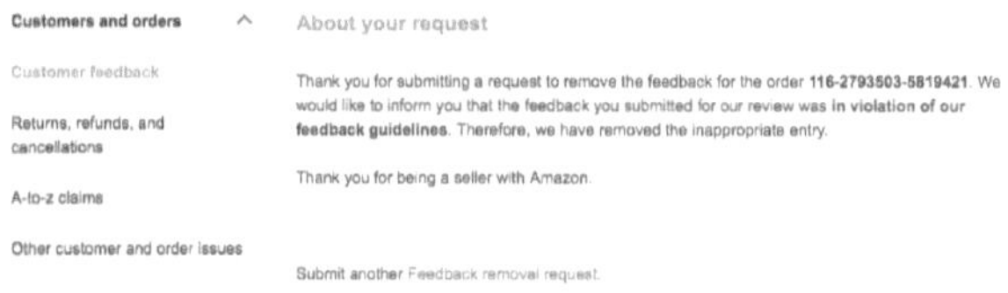

[Image 1.11]

Option 2 – Contact the Customer

Another thing that you can do is to contact the customer and ask them to remove the negative feedback.

Now, be careful because you cannot offer anything in return. It is against Amazon's terms to give a full refund or give anything in exchange for deleting the feedback.

You cannot connect the act of removing the feedback to getting a full refund.

All you can do is apologize for the unsatisfactory service/product and explain what you're doing for it to never happen again. And then humbly ask for them to remove the negative feedback.

Note: The feedback must be removed 60 days from the time they posted it or the feedback won't be eligible for removal after this timeframe.

Sales Boost Idea #8 - Optimal Pricing

It can be difficult to come up with the right price for your product. On one hand, you want to make as much profit as possible. On the other hand, you also don't want it to be super expensive that no one will buy it anymore. So finding the right price for your product may took some trial and error.

I recommend that you follow these steps when optimizing the price of your product:

Step 1 – Get a feel of the market.

The first step is to go to Amazon and just look at your competitors. How much are they selling their product? Is their product offer similar to yours or are they adding something that other seller don't have?

If everyone is selling for $12.99, then you might want to offer yours for $12.49 as a start.

Step 2 – Take note of the 5x rule.

As a general rule, I make sure that I can sell the product for at least 5x the production cost. If it cost me $2 to produce a product per piece, then I must be able to sell it on Amazon for $10. By following the 5x rule, I am giving myself some safety net to still make a decent (20-30%) net profit after all the expenses and FBA fees.

Step 3 – Don't get greedy.

You have to think long-term. Just because you can make an extra $500 per month by increasing your price by $1 doesn't mean you should do it. If you're just starting out and you don't have a lot of reviews yet, I highly recommend that you price your product for as low as possible. You should still be able to make a profit mind you, but in the beginning, the focus should be in getting reviews and building a good reputation for your brand.

Step 4 – Do 14 to 30-day tests.

When you're doing price tests, make sure that you do it in 14 to 30-day timeframes. You cannot possibly get an accurate sales data if you're changing the price every 3 days. Do these tests for 6 months and then look at the data for which price gets the most sales. (Preferably not in December since your data may get skewed by Holiday sales).

Sales Boost Idea #9 - Let Your Customers Ask Questions

Answering customers' questions is a great way to connect with them and it also allows you to remove their doubts before buying your product.

Message some of your customers and let them ask questions about your product. You can also ask a friend of yours to do this and you can show him the most important ones to ask.

Questions should be specific to the product and questions should be about capturing the experience of using the product.

For example:

- How long does this toothbrush last?
- Should I dispose it after 3 months?
- Can I connect an external mic on this camera?
- How long do I need to charge the battery?

Here are some topics that you shouldn't answer:

- Shipping or delivery
- Product availability
- Order specific information
- Customer service

Here are the instructions on asking and answering questions according to Amazon.

How do I ask a question?

On a product page, scroll to the "Customer Questions & Answers" feature. Enter your question in the text box and click "Ask".

How do I answer a question?

To answer questions, click "See all questions & answers" and choose questions you can answer from the "Unanswered questions" feature in the right column.

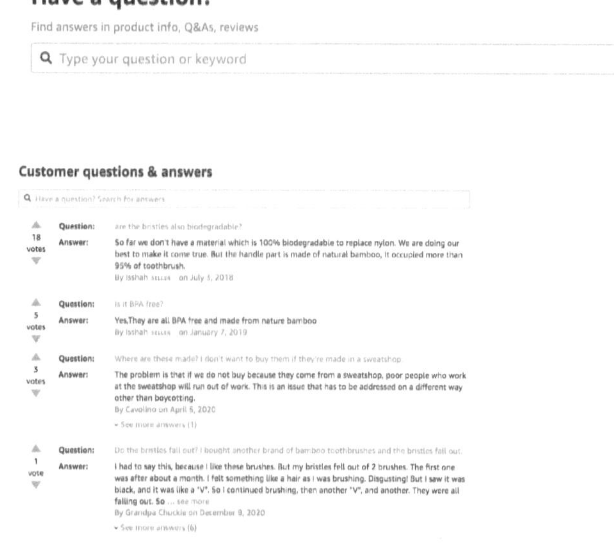

[Image 1.12]

Additional Notes:

A – I highly recommend that you answer as many questions as you can.

B – Go research questions by spying on your competitors. Read their listing, their reviews, and their own Q & A section.

Sales Boost Idea #10 - Apply for Brand Registry

If you want to gain complete control over your Amazon listings, then you have to apply for Brand Registry.

Brand Registry allows you access to enhanced marketing features that Amazon provides. It helps protect a registered trademark and it helps you in having complete control over your brand's image. With Brand Registry, you can add branded products, manage them properly, and eliminate imitation which ensures that your customers are buying legit versions of that product.

Do you remember those super cool and professional product descriptions with text and images? [refer to image 1.13 for an example]. Well those are made via Enhance Brand Content which you can only access if you have Brand Registry.

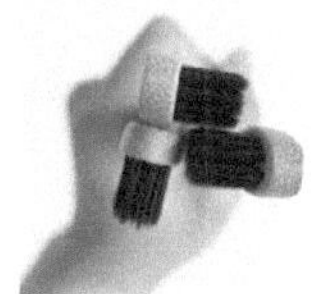

[Image 1.13]

Brand Registry also allows you to win the Buy Box which we will discuss later. There's obviously a ton more benefits but I'm not going to discuss all of those here.

Just know that having **Brand Registry is a MUST.**

Here's how you apply for one:

Step 1 – Check Eligibility Requirements

This will differ from country to country, but the most basic requirements are: A Trademark, a Text-Based Trademark, and an Image-Based Trademark.

Check your requirements here:

https://brandservices.amazon.com/eligibility

Step 2 – Sign Up for Brand Registry

https://brandservices.amazon.com/eligibility

You need to input the following information:

- Give your businesses' information
- Validate your identity via SMS
- Read and accept its policies

Step 3 – Enroll Your Brand/s

Here are the 4 aspects of enrolling a brand:

1 – Brand Eligibility

This consists of your brand name, a few information about your brand, and the number of brand names you want to enroll to Enhance Brand Content (EBC).

2 – Intellectual Property

This includes all the details of your trademark type, trademark name, registering trademark office, and the registration number of your brand.

3 – Identification

This one includes your product images, brand logo/s, packaging images, and website/social media pages.

4 – Characteristics

This one includes your seller account information, vendor account details, barcodes, and manufacturing details like where it is made & distributed.

You have to complete all of these details for you to get approval.

Step 4 – Verification

Wait for 1-2 weeks in which Amazon will forward your brand's details to the registered trademark office. This office will then forward a code to you which you will have to send back to Amazon for verification.

You can do this step by going to:

Amazon Seller Central - > Enter the Respective **Case ID** - > **Go Button**

Select the **Respond or View Button** - > **Choose Reply** - > Paste the Code and click **Send.**

If you need more help on getting approved, I highly recommend that you contact Amazon's support as I found them to be really helpful for this process.

Sales Boost Idea #11 - Win Amazon's Buy Box

Around 83% of all Amazon sales comes through the Buy Box. That means, if you're not winning the Buy Box, then you're not really making a killing with your product. Which also means winning the buy box is equal to getting 5x more sales than what you usually make.

If you're not familiar with the buy box, it's basically the Add to Cart and the Buy Button on the right side of an Amazon listing. If you look further down on that part, you will most likely see other vendors selling the same product you are selling.

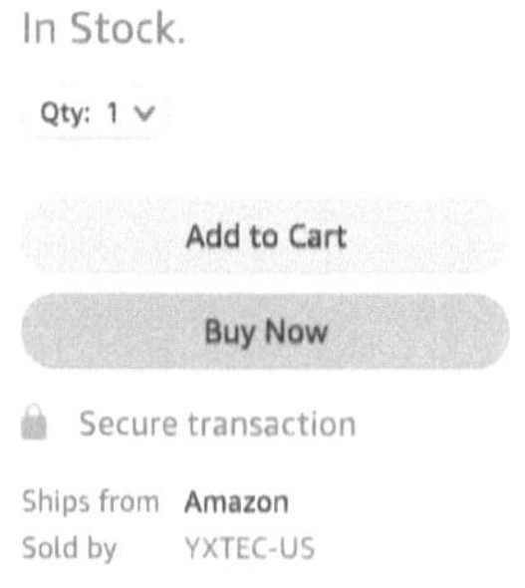

[Image 1.14]

(This particular buy box was won by YXTEC-US)

[Image 1.15]

(The other 6 sellers are available but only 17% of people on average look at them)

83% of the people who will buy the product won't even consider looking at the other vendors available. They will most likely purchase from the one who already has the buy box.

So how do you win the buy box? What are the things that you can do so Amazon will favor you as the winner?

A – Inventory

You should always replenish your inventory on time. The less problems you have with inventory availability, the better your chances of getting the buy box.

B - Fast Shipping

Fast shipping is a necessity these days. People are not willing to wait for more than 5 days anymore. Make sure that your items always arrive on time.

C - Customer-Service

You must also have an impeccable & prompt customer service. Answer any questions that they may have and always be polite when talking to customers.

D - Use of FBA/Professional Seller Account

You must have a professional seller's account or you'll have almost no chance of getting the buy box. Also, using FBA helps you with the last 2 metrics (fast shipping and customer service) since Amazon will do those 2 for you.

E - Competitive Pricing

Remember Amazon's mission: **To provide the widest selection at the lowest price.** That means Amazon wants you to provide cheaper prices compared to the competition.

F – Brand Registry/Enhance Brand Content

Registering for Brand Registry also helps in letting Amazon know that your brand and the products you sell are of the highest quality in the market.

G – Seller Rating

Amazon has 0 to 11 seller rating system and the higher your rating is, the more likely you are to get the buy box.

You cannot really control this one, so all you can do is try to provide the best product and respond to customers' inquiries as fast as possible.

Also, make sure that you have less than 1% product defect rate so you won't get penalized by Amazon.

***

There are obviously no guarantees when it comes to Amazon's decisions, but the more you follow these 7 key aspects, the better your chances of winning the buy box.

Sales Boost Idea #12 - Classify Your Products in the Right Category

Did you know that customers are 8.9% more likely to buy a product if they're in the right category? True story. I mean, Amazon said so.

Here's a shortcut in making sure that your product is in its right classification/category.

Look at your competitors' category and copy them.

If you're selling some kinesiology tape, then find your closest competitors and just look at what category they are using.

[Image 1.16]

Just copy the categories that they are using and classify your products on the same category inside your Seller Central Account.

Amazon will also automatically recommend other categories that you might want to use.

You can use Amazon's product classifier here:

https://sellercentral.amazon.com/hz/inventory/classify

Here are the instructions directly from Amazon (I'm putting it here for your convenience):

Step 1: Select your products' classifications

Go to the Product Classifier tool and use either the Browse or Search method to identify the appropriate classifications for your products.

Browse

1. Select the store in which your product belongs.
2. Continue to narrow the classification options until the Select button appears.
3. Click Select to add the classification to your list.
4. Repeat the process to classify all of your products.
5. Click Download List, and save the file.

Search

1. Type a keyword into the Search box.
2. Click the "+" (plus) sign to the left of the category name to select classifications for your products.
3. Repeat the process to classify all of your products.
4. Click Download List, and save the file.

[Image 1.17]

Step 2: Download the inventory file template

To identify the correct Inventory File Template:

1. Open the Product Classifier file and identify the inventory file template for your products by reviewing the suggestions in the Inventory Template Name column.
2. Go to Inventory File Templates, and download and save the inventory file or files. You can use more than one inventory file.

   Note: For sellers using XML feeds, you can use an XML upload.

Step 3: Populate the classification and refinement fields

To add your selected classifications and refinements to your inventory file template files:

Classification

1. Open the Product Classifier file, and scroll to the Fields Required for Classification columns: Classification Field and Valid Values columns.
2. Identify the Classification Field for one of the products you are listing.
3. Identify these same fields in your inventory file template.

   Note: item_type_keyword in the Product Classifier file corresponds to item_type in the Inventory File Template and the ItemType attribute in XML files

4. Copy the Valid Values from the Product Classifier file into the corresponding cell in the inventory file template for the product

[Image 1.18]

4. Copy the Valid Values from the Product Classifier file into the corresponding cell in the inventory file template for the product you are listing.

5. Repeat this process for all of the products you are listing.

Refinement:

1. Open the Product Classifier file, and scroll to the Refinements columns: Refinement Name, Refinement Field, Valid Values, and Modifier.

2. Identify the Refinement Field for one of the products you are listing.

3. Identify these same fields in your inventory file template.

4. Copy the Valid Values from the Product Classifier file into the corresponding cell in the inventory file template for the product you are listing.

5. Repeat this process for all of the products you are listing.

[Image 1.19]

You can also find it here:

https://sellercentral.amazon.com/gp/help/external/201576420

Sales Boost Idea #13 - Use Fulfillment by Amazon

I know, this may have been the most obvious sales boost idea in this book. But if you're still not using FBA by now, then the first thing that you have to do is to put down this book, go to your Seller Central account and sign-up for the FBA program.

The FBA program is probably the most genius thing ever when it comes to e-commerce. With FBA, I don't have to worry about shipping the product to the individual and I also don't have to worry about customer service since Amazon will take care of this for me. This saves me so much time that I can spend with my family and other parts of my business as well.

Sure, you have to pay some fees but it's well worth the investment because Amazon can ship so much faster than what I can do as an individual. When it comes to e-commerce, FAST SHIPPING is one of the keys to success and Amazon has the capability to do it the fastest.

If you want to know the nitty gritty on how you can find suppliers and ship your product to Amazon's warehouse, then I highly recommend that you check out my book FBA Product Sourcing Blueprint.

https://www.amazon.com/gp/product/B08NNTXHM9

Part 2

Product Based Ideas

Sales Boost Idea #14 - Sell Other Products and Establish a Brand

If you want to make as much money as possible, then you have to sell other products as well. Think of your product line up as an army of brand evangelists. A few months ago, I bought a body wash from a semi-unknown brand and mygod, I freaking love it. Can you guess what I did next? I checked out all their other lineups from shampoo, shaving cream, facewash, etc. I was so happy with one of their products that I decided to use that brand exclusively.

Imagine if I searched for their brand and the only product they are selling is that one body wash? I would've been disappointed because I really love the first product that I bought from them.

Obviously, in the beginning, you cannot have a product line up – but once you started growing, the next step is to expand and create and sell other products related to your first one.

This is how you build a successful e-commerce brand. You create one great product after another and then you dominate your market one new loyal customer at a time.

KEYS TO REMEMBER:

#1 – Sell Other Related/Complementary Products

Your next products should be complementary products that your original customers can buy. If you're selling a bamboo toothbrush, then sell a bamboo toothbrush case. If you're selling shampoo for men, then sell body wash for men for your next one.

#2 – Bundle Your Products

Another thing that you can do is to create a bundle and sell your products as a set. This will increase your average order and profit at the same time.

#3 – Great/Differentiated Product is Key

At the end of the day, your product must do what it promises to do. The only reason I got converted as a customer is because I love the first product that I bought. This is the key to your success with e-commerce, you must have a product with added value. If not, then you're just going to be a copycat and you will be out of business by this time next year.

Sales Boost Idea #15 - Drive Reviews and Customer Loyalty with Product Inserts

Getting more reviews is one of the most important type of marketing that you could ever do. More reviews mean more social proof that you have a great product. This is where product inserts come in. Aside from reviews, there's also a ton more other benefits that you could get from using them as well.

A product insert is basically a card (or a piece of paper) that you put inside the package that acts as an additional marketing material.

The intention is to communicate something with your customers. And that something could be the following:

1 – Get Feedback/Reviews. Customer reviews will always be the lifeblood of our products. Without them, we won't have any social proof that shows that our product is the best in the market.

2 – Customer Appreciation. You can also show appreciation for purchasing your product by simply saying "Thank You" or putting some kind of heartfelt message to your customers.

3 – Discount Codes. Offering discount codes via insert cards is a surefire way to get additional sales.

4 – Additional Instructions. If you're product is a little complicated or it require some additional instructions, an

insert is where you could put that additional text so they can maximize the use of the product.

5 – Promote Other Products. You can also mention other products that you have via an insert card, although in this case, you might want to put a bigger one instead of your classic 3 x 5 or 4 x 6 ones.
Note - Remember that you cannot do the following when it comes to product inserts:

1 – You cannot promote websites. NEVER re-direct your customers to your website. If you're going to promote a product, make sure that you mention that they should go to your Amazon store.

2 – Do not offer discounts and ask for reviews at the same time. NEVER offer discount codes and ask for a review at the same time. For your insert card, you can either ask for a sale via a discount code or you can ask for a review instead. You cannot combine them together in just one card.

3 – Do not use low quality papers. Your customers care about what you put in the package. Low quality papers easily get crumpled which makes the card looks less appealing.

4 – Do not divert the customers outside Amazon except if it's your social media properties like Facebook page or Instagram account.

5 – Do not specifically ask for a "positive/5-star review." This is against Amazon's TOS as well.

Here are some examples of awesome product inserts:

[Image 1.17]

[Image 1.18]

[Image 1.19]

Always err on the safe side. Yes, you can probably get away from incentivizing reviews, offering discounts for reviews, and re-directing customers to your website but I personally wouldn't risk it.

Whenever you're in doubt, always read Amazon's updated Terms of Service.

https://sellercentral.amazon.com/gp/help/G200386250

Sales Boost Idea #16 - Drive Sales with Product Inserts

Another awesome benefit of a product insert is you can drive additional sales from customers who already love you (assuming of course that you have a good product).

Here's how you can drive more sales through product inserts.

Step 1 – Thank You Message. Most seller just put a simple "Thank You" message and in most cases, that's actually pretty fine already. However, if you want to take it to the next level – adding a 2-3 sentence message saying how much you appreciate their support and how their patronage means a lot to your family owned business.

Step 2 – Mention Other Related Products. After saying thank you, you can then mention other related products that your store has.

Step 3 – Ask Them to Go to Your Amazon Store and Mention Your Brand.

Step 4 – Offer a Discount Code. Make sure that this code is only limited to 1 per customer.

In most cases, combining Step 1 and Step 4 is enough to get an increase of 20% in your sales every month.

Example of a good product insert that drive sales:

[Image 1.20]

As you can see on image 1.20, you can use the left one to drive sales, and then the right one to drive reviews. I wouldn't put them on one package as that may be in the gray area of Amazon's term of service.

The example on the left is probably the best example I can give when It comes to driving additional sales. It's simple, it's clean and it's direct to the point.

Here are more awesome ones to copy:

[Image 1.21]

[Image 1.22]

[Image 1.23]

Key things to remember:

1 – Do not direct your customers to your email, funnel, website or any web properties outside Amazon.com. Your social media pages are perfectly fine.

2 – You can offer a discount code but remember not to ask for a review at the same time. This is against Amazon's TOS.

Sales Boost Idea #17 - Offer Product Differentiation (Value Skewing)

I want to introduce you to the concept of value-skewing. It's basically about adding value to a product by being different and by giving what the customers are asking for. By adding value to the product, you'll be able to increase your sales and make your customers happy at the same time. It's a win-win situation for you and your customers.

Here's How to Differentiate via Value-Skewing:

1 – Materials and/or Ingredients.

You can use, not only better and higher quality ingredients but also materials and ingredients that your customers value. For example, if your customers are "ingredients sensitive" – they might prefer stevia over sugar. Stevia is healthier and it's a great substitute for sugar. In this case, changing an ingredient increases the value of your product in your customers eyes.

2 – Colors.

Adding different colors increases their options. There's a reason why the iPhone has different hues and colors for their devices. It's good for business and the customers want variety of options.

3 – Sizes.

Another way to add value is by adding sizes. There's no such thing as one size fits all. One t-shirt size cannot fit us all. One shoe size isn't enough. Offer different sizes and you'll be able to cater to a wider audience.

4 - Additional Features (via Research).

This will depend on the type of product you are selling. But there's always that one or two feature that customers are always looking for on a specific product. The best way to find these features is to read Amazon reviews and discover what customers are actually asking for.

5 – Origin.

Most of the time, the origin/manufacturing country of the product is a value-add in itself. There's a reason why Made in America or Made in Italy or Made in "Insert Country Here" matters in customers' buying decision.
But this still depends on the type of product you are selling. The general rule here is "the more expensive the product is, the better it is if it's *made in U.S.A., other Western Countries + Highly Reputable Manufacturing countries like Japan*" – and I'm not saying this because it's 100% true all of the time. I'm saying this because this is what the customers ASSUME (in general). The truth is, a product made from China can have higher quality than a product made in the U.S. However, this is not the current narrative that the market believes. Until this change, the origin of a product will continue to have an impact on customers' product preferences.

6 – Branding.

Another way to differentiate is through branding. By having a compelling story for your brand, you'll be able to change your customer's perception of your product. Branding is a complicated topic and I can write a whole book about it. But when it comes to e-commerce branding, the most important stuff are the following:

A – Always use social proof. This could be in the form of product reviews and/or endorsement from reputable users.
B – Start using video in your marketing.
C – Having the highest quality product is *branding done right* in itself.

7 – Packaging.

Your product's packaging affects how your product is seen in the market. Always use high quality materials in your packaging and try to give them an unboxing experience if possible. Look at what Apple is doing in their products, there's a reason why unboxing videos are getting millions of views online – customers love a good unboxing experience!

8 – Bonuses/Add-ons/Bundle.

Customers want more options so adding some kind of bonus/add-ons or even bundling a product can add profit to your bottom-line. Add-ons are always a good idea as long as it is actually adding value to what the customers are purchasing.

We will discuss some of these in detail on the next few chapters... Keep reading!

Sales Boost Idea #18 - Offer Purchase Add-ons + Multi-Packs

Remember that the best add-ons are complementary products.

For example, if you're selling a shaving razor then you might want to sell other products related to the razor.

As an example, let's look at what SHAVING REVOLUTION offers…

https://www.amazon.com/s?k=SHAVING+REVOLUTION

This company also offers: Double Edge Safety Razor, Stand, Bowl, After-Shave Balm, Pre-Shave Oil, and Badger Brush.

By having an add-on of other products that complements the original purchase, they can easily increase their sales and profit margin.

Remember that it's easier to sell to a customer that is already sold in the idea of buying one of your products. In this case, offering other stuff that may enhance their experience is in fact, not only more profitable but is also the right thing to do.

MULTI-PACKS

You can also offer what we call "multi-packs" and sell them by the number. 1 Pack, 2 Packs, 3 Packs, and so on are the usual. For example, instead of selling 1-piece of shaving soap, you can offer 5 pieces in 1-pack. And then you can do 2-packs, 3-packs and so on. The appeal of a pack is they can save money by buying bulk plus they don't have to worry about shipping fees over and over again. Try this simple strategy and see the results for yourself!

Sales Boost Idea #19 - Offer Gift Wrapping Options

Okay, technically – you're not really going to get a share of the profit for gift wrapping – but you should still offer it and enable it on Amazon.

Why? Because it offers a better customer buying experience. A lot of people buy products because they want to give it as a gift to someone they care about, and a lot of them also want the option to have it gift wrap. Remember, happy wife, happy life – oh wait – that's a different book – just change "wife" to "customers" and it's still true!

The actual price of the gift wrap will depend on how big the item is but you don't really have to worry about this since the customers will shoulder the cost for it.

If you're in FBA, then Amazon will automatically offer this service for your product. If it isn't, then you can go to your Seller Central account and go to **Settings**, then click **Gift Options**.

Click Edit next to **Gift** Messaging or **Gift-Wrap**, then enable the service for individual order items. Click Continue to save the setting.

[Image 1.24]
[Image from Gorillaroi*]

Sales Boost Idea #20 - Read Competitors' Product Reviews and Improve Based on Customer Feedback

If you want to maximize the effect of value-skewing, then you have to know what your customers' most valued features [want and need] on a specific product. The best way to do this is to read your competitors' product reviews on Amazon and take note of what the customers are saying – both the positive and the negative stuff.

Let's say that you want to sell your own brand of Single-Blade Razor.

Here are the steps that I would take to research this product.

Step 1 – Search on Amazon.

I'll search for my closest competitors by searching for keywords like:

Single edge razor

Single blade razor

Step 2 – Read the Q & A section to find out customers' concerns.

When you read the Q & A section, try to find questions that appears over and over again on different products. By doing this, you'll know exactly what the common concerns are when it comes to this type of product.

In this case, I found the following concerns to be important for this market:

A – Where is the razor made? (major concern for this market*)

B – How many shaves can you get from one blade? (the more the better)

C – Does it come with blades? (they don't want to spend money on a razor that doesn't come with free blades)

By reading the Q & A section of different listings, I'd get to have an idea of their major concerns when buying a single edge razor.

Step 3 – Read the 1-star to 2-star reviews and find out about their concerns and what they didn't like about the product.

Step 4 – Read the 4 to 5-star reviews and find out what they like about the product.

Step 5 – Create a list and collect these concerns/comments.

Make sure that you put all your research into one document so you can refer to it as you source your product.

Step 6 – Create a better product that solves their concerns.

This is where all the research comes into fruition.

In order to create a product that gives you the best chance of winning the market, you have to solve the problems that you found on your research.

If your potential customers hate "China made razor", can you offer on that is locally made? Would it still make sense financially speaking? If yes, then this is a value-skew that you can turn in your favor.

If your customers prefer a single edge razor with matte grippable razor, can you offer this to them as an added value for your product?

This is not just about one feature, it's about adding value stack after another so you can become the preferred solution for your market's problems.

All of these starts with a simple product research on Amazon.

Sales Boost Idea #21 - Offer Different Product Colors and/or Sizes

This is probably the easiest value-skew that you can do since it doesn't really take that much effort on your part.

Customers will always have different preferences and needs when it comes to colors and sizes. There's a reason why there's different sizes of shoes, t-shirts, mobile devices, etc.

We want and need variety because there's no one size fits all.

When it comes to colors and sizes, you can try to go against the grain or just go with the flow.

For example, if you're selling a t-shirt, then people would expect that you'll have the classic colors like white, back, and grey.

If you're selling an aluminum razor, then you should probably have the classic matte or the mirror polished one. Then you can also use different touches like rose gold, jet black, and matte black to add a little flair to your product.

When it comes to color, try to follow the current trend if possible. For example, "rose gold" and "matte black" has been a big hit for Apple in the past few years and these colors had been ingrained to us as cool and hip. If possible, try to incorporate these colors to your products so you can have something attractive to offer your customers.

Sales Boost Idea #22 - Offer Bundles

This is one of my top value-skew to offer. Why?

Because it's a value-skew that helps you make more profit and makes your customers' save money at the same time.

When it comes to bundles, always think about what the customers need aside from your main product. Think about products that will complement your main one.

If you're selling a premium razor, then you may want to sell shaving cream, post shave oil, a brush, moisturizer, face wash, etc.

[Image 1.25]

Another bundle idea I recommend is the "Bundle 1 2 3 Strategy"

Instead of putting all of your available products in just 1 big bundle, you can create different types of bundles that will give your customers more options.

For example, Supplyco offers a "Starter Kit" with the razor, shaving cream, post shave healing, and shaving brush. That is bundle #1.

[Image 1.26]

But they also offer other smaller bundles that includes some of the same products, which we can call bundle #2 and bundle #3.

Obviously, you can change the name with something cooler but you get the point. ☺

See the image below for an example.

[Image 1.27]

Note: When it comes to the number of unique items inside your biggest bundle, I recommend that you put no more than 6 items inside. For your smaller bundles, 2-3 items per bundle is the usual practice.

Sales Boost Idea #23 - Offer Premium Product Options

There is a market for cheap and affordable items, just like there will always be a market for premium products.

So how would I approach this?

I would personally create a different brand if I offer a lot of other premium products. However, if it's only 1 or 2 items, I would just put it under the same brand. This will automatically increase the value of my other "cheaper" products.

Let's say that you are selling a mid-priced $50 razor. You can come up with a more expensive razor at the price range of $150-$200. Now, you shouldn't expect to make a lot of sales for this one but you can still make a decent profit from it. At the same time, this also increases the value of your cheaper products. Most people can't afford a $200 razor, so they would go for the next best thing which is your cheaper, but still perfectly awesome $50 alternative.

This is what Zafirro did with their razors (although this one is to the total extreme).

They offered a razor made of gold for $18,000 and one made of iridium for $100,000.

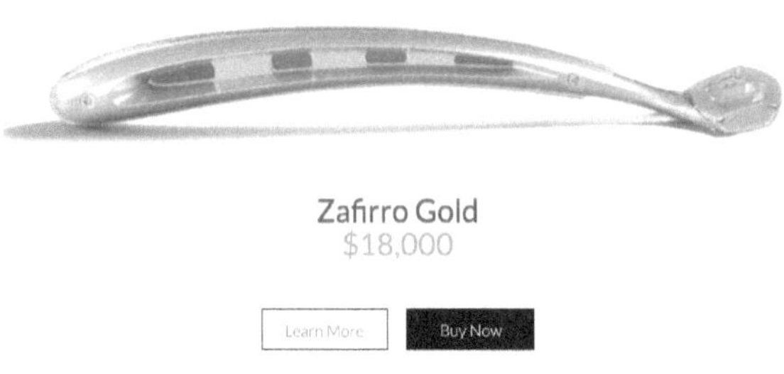

[Image 1.28]

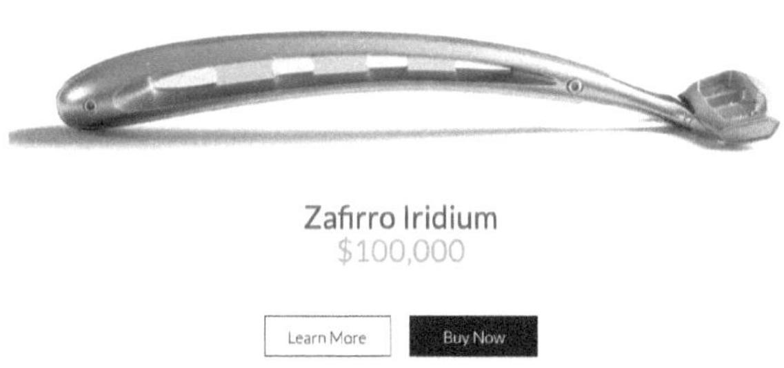

[Image 1.29]

Then they offer the "Zafirro Z2" at $199 which is still quite expensive for a razor. But because of their 2 other products, $199 seems like a bargain now in comparison to their original offerings.

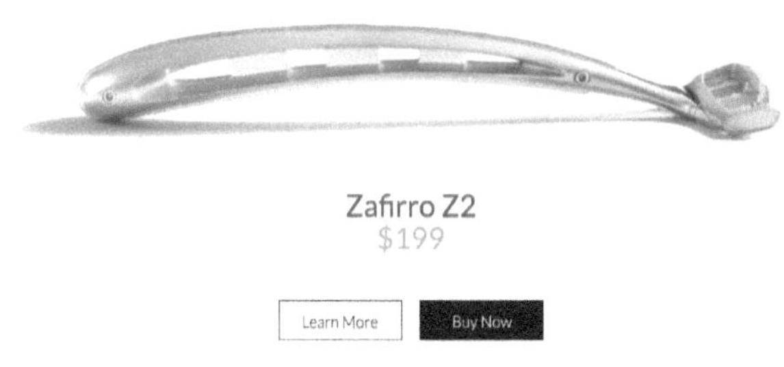

[Image 1.30]

You don't have to source thousands of your premium product, a few hundred (especially in the beginning) will do.

Honestly, it doesn't really take more effort to sell a more expensive product. You can pretty much use the same tactics that you learned from this book so far. The only major difference is you'll probably have to advertise and promote a little bit more than usual.

That's where the next part comes in. Marketing and Promotion are key aspects of every business, especially the ones that are still trying to make a name for their brands.

Now, remember that these advertising and promotion techniques are all useless if you don't have a good product and if you didn't optimize your Amazon listing for maximum sales. Focus on those 2 aspects first before you dive right into ads and promotions.

Part 3

Marketing & Promotion

Sales Boost Idea #24 - Advertise on Amazon

Okay, first of all I'm not going to teach you the technical aspect of advertising on Amazon here. You can learn that easy peasy stuff through Amazon's blog: https://advertising.amazon.com/en-us/blog.

What I want to teach you are the most important stuff that you have to remember when you're advertising on Amazon. Think of these as the best practices to follow when you start advertising your products. The more of these you follow, the more likely you are to gain higher profits.

MY TOP 7 AMAZON ADS BEST PRACTICES:

#1 - Start with $3-$5 Budget Per Day

You don't have to start with $20 or even $50 per day budget. The first 3-4 weeks of your ads should be spent testing campaigns and finding out what works. Not all of us have thousands of dollars for an ad campaign, but we can all run 3-4 campaigns at $3 per day per campaign.

#2 – Start with 3 Ads (Manual and Automatic)

When you start running ads, DO NOT try to run different ad creatives or copy. Just create one ad copy and make the AUDIENCE your key variable.

That means running 1 automatic campaign, 1 manual with all your main keywords, and another one with all your broad keywords. You should run these campaigns for 2-3 weeks without changing anything.

#3 – Use Your Keyword List

A keyword list is basically a master file that consists of all the keywords that you can use for your listing so you can rank higher on Amazon's search engine. You can also use these keywords for Amazon ads and Google ads. If you don't have this master keyword list yet, I recommend that you check out the 3rd part of this series called Amazon Keyword Research.

As a starter, I recommend that you gather your main keywords by searching for products related to yours on Amazon and then grab the keywords that are most related to what you're selling.

#4 – Use Amazon Dynamic Bids – Down Only

Always start with this bidding option so you don't overpay for ads.

#5 – Start with Amazon's Bid Recommendation and Don't Change Anything for 2 Weeks

For the amount of bid, start with what Amazon recommends and then don't change anything for two weeks. Amazon's algorithm takes time and changing things brings confusion to the system. Just stick with what you already have and **let the machines do the work**. Out of the 3 campaigns that you got, one will likely be a clear winner after 2-3 weeks and you'll know which ad audience works best for you.

#6 – Don't Stop the Campaign if 1-2 Sales Can Put You in the Green

If 1 or 2 sales will put you to positive ROI, then don't stop the campaign just yet. Keep running it for another week or two and see if it will turn itself around. Most of my successful campaigns didn't start profitable. They all need that time so Amazon can find the best audience for my product.

#7 – Scale by Duplicating Profitable Campaigns

Once you found that winning/profitable campaign, do not scale the ad by 5x'ing your budget. If you're running a $5 per day ad, then you should only max out the per day budget up to $20. You should scale instead by creating a similar campaign with only 1 tiny difference. I recommend that you change just one thing and then start running that ad as well. Most of the time, I'll just remove 1 or 2 keywords that are spending but not really making any profit.

Sales Boost Idea #25 - Use Facebook Ads

The great thing about Facebook Ads is you can target via a specific demographic or interests. In addition, you can collect email address that you can use for your long-term ecommerce success. And even more awesome is you can test different ad creatives like images and videos. In short, you're not limited unlike on Amazon.

So, should you directly send customers to your Amazon Listing?

Frankly, I do not recommend it. Amazon ads can get expensive if your product doesn't have the best profit margin. In this case, you have to play the long game and get as many emails as you can while also selling the product at the same time.

Here's the strategy I recommend:

Ad - > Landing Page - > Listing

Start with a Facebook Ad, send them to a landing page with a discount coupon, and then send them to your Amazon listing after they signed up for the discount code. With this strategy, you'll be able to collect their email and send them to your listing at the same time.

My Ad Recommendation:

VIDEO WORKS BEST. A simple 1-minute video showcasing your product's features and benefits is the best type of ad you can do right now.

Check out these links for an example:

DishFish:
https://www.youtube.com/watch?v=umnz-4ZlrEc&ab_channel=DishFish%E2%84%A2

Recurve Bows:
https://www.youtube.com/watch?v=4B12pqCX7LY&ab_channel=Camping%26Hiking

Roof Cleaner:
https://www.youtube.com/watch?v=OAxlRWHL-Vo&ab_channel=30SecondsLtd

MY TARGETING RECOMMENDATION:

Start with your main market. Use your common sense and market knowledge here. Who are your main customers? Are they men or women? Where do they live? What type of fan pages are they following on Facebook? You have to know these things and I would assume that you already did your research because you are already selling something in your chosen market.

My Landing Page Recommendation:

[Image 1.31]

For your landing page, I recommend a simple one that clearly mention what they are getting.

Start with the headline that says "Save Big on X [your product]"

Add a picture on the left side. Then on the right side, tell them exactly how much they are saving, plus add the button that lets them sign up for the coupon code.

You can use any of these landing page creators: WordPress (free), Leadpages, Clickfunnels, or Unbounce.

Once they signed up, send them the coupon code via email and then direct them to your Amazon listing so they could buy the product.

Sales Boost Idea #26 - Use Instagram to Increase Market Share

Instagram is still one of the most underutilized platform when it comes to e-commerce. The goal for Instagram marketing isn't really to make quick-sales, the goal should be about building a brand people love and trust.

So, this isn't exactly a "quick sales boost idea."

Nonetheless, I still recommend that you create a brand that is active on Instagram because it will separate your products from the thousands of competitors that you have.

You already know that when it comes to Instagram, high-quality images are the key. That's pretty obvious. But what are you supposed to have other than that?

#1 – Use Variety of Content

Always go for variety of content. You can post about your products directly promoting them, you can post a quote related to your product, a customer testimonial, fun facts, behind the scenes, and other video content. The key here is to post as much variety as you can.

#2 – Encourage User-Generated Content

This one is going to play a major role in your brand's ability to dominate a market. Just about every brand that is killing it on Instagram right now are using user-generated content. Always encourage your customers to post your product on Instagram, and then re-post them so you can use it as content. Being featured makes your customers appreciate your brand more thus making them an evangelist for your products.

#3 – Use the Right Hashtags

Don't just use random hashtags that has nothing to do with your post. Always research the most important ones that are related to what you're sharing. There's nothing more annoying to an IG user than finding images of non-related pictures when they're searching for a hashtag they like to explore.

#4 – Interact with Your Followers

Lastly, you want to interact with your followers as much as possible. In the beginning, I recommend that you like and reply every single comment that you will get on your page. This is going to be harder once you already have thousands of followers but you should still do it as much as possible. Replying on comments differentiates you from the corporate pirates who only cares about their profits. Be different and actually take the time to create even a small connection with your customers.

Sales Boost Idea #27 - Find & Work with Influencers

I know, I know… everyone seems like an influencer nowadays and it is hard to find someone who can truly be a good influencer for your brand.

Here's what I recommend that you do:

Step 1 – Know Who Your Audience Is

You have to know who your audience is. What hashtags are they following? What type of videos are they watching? What type of content are they into? Knowing exactly what type of stuff your audience is into will maximize the effect of an influencer (even the ones with only 5,000 to 30,000 followers).

Step 2 – Find the Right Medium

The next step is to choose the right medium. What's the best platform that you can use in order to achieve your goals? This will depend on what you want. Do you want to increase brand awareness? Do you want to get as much sales as possible? Create the right expectation so you can achieve the most desirable results. Then choose a platform that would best serve your intentions. You can choose between Instagram, TikTok, YouTube, Twitter, or Facebook.

Step 3 – Find and Work with the Right Influencer

To find influencers to work with, I recommend that you use BuzzSumo's influencer search tool.

https://buzzsumo.com/find-influencers/

There's a 30-day free trial and that should be enough time for you to find awesome influencers you can work with.
If you have a relatively new brand and you don't have a big budget yet, I recommend that you focus on working with micro-influencers. These are influencers with 10k to 50k followers. They're cheaper and they will have higher conversions than those who already have hundreds of thousands of followers. Most micro-influencers will charge between $50 to $500 per post. So, before you choose the ones you want to work with, make sure that you check the following first:

A – Engagement. They should be active in interacting with their followers.
B – Specialization. You should choose someone who clearly specialize on the type of product you want to promote.
C – Reach. Go for the ones with less than 50,000 followers if you're just getting started with Influencer marketing.

I highly recommend that you check-out this informative article about the ins and outs of Influencer marketing:

https://influencermarketinghub.com/influencer-rates/

Step 4 – Track Your Campaigns

Always use some kind of unique coupon or trackable unique link so you know exactly how many people are buying your product through the Influencer's recommendation. A discount code is my go-to option since they're much easier to track.

Sales Boost Idea #28 - Use Amazon's Early Reviewer Program

We all know the importance of Amazon product reviews by now.

More reviews, means more social proof, which typically leads to more sales. And no product reviews, means no sales, and no sales means you don't get any reviews – it's the classic what comes first? Egg or chicken.

So how in the world can you get reviews?

Remember, you cannot purchase or exchange reviews – that would be against Amazon's Terms of Service.

This is where **Amazon Early Reviewer Program** comes in.

What it does is it allows you to get at least 5 initial reviews for your brand-new product.

But first, you have to find out if you are eligible for the program.

Here are some of the requirements according to Amazon:

- The product must be for sale on Amazon.com or Amazon.co.uk
- You have to have a brand registry
- The product must have less than 5 reviews when you apply for the program
- The product cost must be at least $15
- It must have its own SKU barcode

The Price

Is it worth the $60 that you have to pay for? I believe so. A product that has at least 5 reviews is 2.5x more likely to get sales than the one without any.

Go on and apply your product to the Early Reviewer Program because it's the best $60 you'll ever spend this week.

*To **participate**, submit your product via 'Seller Central > Advertising > **Early Reviewer Program**'. You can submit single SKUs directly via the **Amazon Early Reviewer Program** dashboard.*

Sales Boost Idea #29 - Apply for Lightning Deals

Doing an Amazon Lightning Deal is one of the best ways to gain market visibility and increase your product sales on Amazon. It also allows you to get a leap against the competition and it gives you the chance to sustain it by increasing your best-seller rankings.

Amazon Lightning Deals are pretty straightforward. You apply to be included in a lightning deal, Amazon promotes the deal, and your product gets discounted for no more than 6 hours.

Eligibility

Here are the requirements for approval:

- You must be a "professional" seller
- Your product must be receiving at least 5 reviews per month
- You must have a seller rating of at least 3.5 stars
- The product must have an average rating of at least 3 stars
- A product with variations is a plus
- Your product shouldn't be in the non-eligible categories like e-cigarettes, medical devices, alcohol, and adult products

How to Apply for a Lightning Deal

Log-in to your Seller Central panel - > Select the Create tab - > Pick the One You Want a Deal for - > click Edit - >

fill the needed information like schedule, minimum price, and minimum deal quantity.

You can monitor the status of your application through the Lightning Deal Dashboard.

The fee to join varies, but the average would be around $150. It's definitely worth the price since you'll be getting an avalanche of sales plus this would be great for your product in the long-term.

Think of the sales for the deal as a bonus.

The real benefit of lightning deals is you'll get the chance to get more sales after the deal since your product will have a much higher best-seller ranking and more people will see and buy from your listing.

Sales Boost Idea #30 - Make Your Products Amazon Prime Eligible

Consider prime as a gift from the e-commerce gods, or maybe Jeff Bezos – who knows. All I know is that being an Amazon Prime eligible seller is awesome!

For the buyer, they get free shipping, discounts and other promos.

For the sellers, you will get a prime badge which is crucial nowadays on Amazon. It means you're in the cool club with the cool kids – and in this case, the cool kids are buying a lot of stuff on Amazon.

How to Join Amazon Prime:

Option #1 - Self-Fulfilled Prime. If you store and ship your own products, you can still join prime via SFP. You need to join the waitlist at the moment since they're not openly accepting members.

You'll be put into a trial mode and you're going to have to perform tasks that is up to par to their standards.

You can join the waitlist here:

https://sell.amazon.com/programs/seller-fulfilled-prime.html

Option #2 - Join Amazon FBA. If you're already an FBA seller, then you don't have to worry anymore. All you have

to do is maintain a good seller performance rating and you're in!
(https://sellercentral.amazon.com/gp/help/external/G200 205250?language=en_US)

This is still the easiest way to be prime eligible, plus the fees are basically baked into your Amazon selling fees so you don't need to worry about that as well.

Joining Amazon Prime is probably the least effort activity you can do to increase your sales. This should be priority #1 as soon as you start selling your products on Amazon.

Sales Boost Idea #31 - Join Amazon's Subscribe & Save Program

Think of the Subscribe and Save program as Amazon's digital loyalty card. People get to save money by subscribing and you get to make consistent sales and profit by having subscriptions on the products you are selling.

This works best for products that are sold on a weekly/monthly basis. Products like food, toiletries, health products and most consumable stuff.

How to Join Subscribe and Save Program

Step 1 – Go to your FBA account's settings.

Step 2 – Locate **Subscription & Settings** and **Enable Subscribe and Save.**

Step 3 – Add the products that you want to include.

And voila! You're ready to sell your product subscription!

What I like about the S&S program is it runs forever. It's not liked a one-time lightning deal. With S&S, you get to do this thing once and you get to benefit from it forever.

In terms of long-term income, this is one of the best things you can do for your Amazon business.

Note: Check out this link below for some eligibility requirements

https://sellercentral.amazon.com/gp/help/external/G2016
20110?language=en_US

Sales Boost Idea #32 - Post Your Listing on Your Personal FB Profile

Okay, this may seem like a trivial thing to do but if you're just getting started – you must do everything in your power to promote your products. And that includes sharing them on your Facebook profile.

A simple post sharing the link of your product/s will do. Let your friends know that your company produces these products and ask them to check it out if it's something that they want or need.

That's it. Simple, but actually quite effective for getting a few sales every now and then.

Sales Boost Idea #33 - Expand to International Markets

Amazon Global Selling is definitely not for everyone. However, if you have a product that is selling quite well in the U.S., then there's a good chance that it could be a hit for other markets as well. Obviously, there are no guarantees since every market is different, but it wouldn't hurt to try and sell your best-selling product on international marketplaces.

I recommend that you start with Amazon.co.uk since Western culture will still be prevalent in this region and you'll still have almost the same demographic for your product.

The process is pretty much the same, except that you'll send your products on Amazon's international warehouse instead.

You can register for a UK seller central account here:

https://sellercentral.amazon.co.uk/

Some things to remember before you sell your products on Amazon UK:

1 – Check the legal implications and regulations of selling internationally.

2 – Check out your competition to know the average price of your product in the international scene.

3 – Always start small and test 20 to 100 pieces of your product first before you go all-in.

P.S. I will probably be writing a book about International markets like UK and Japan in the near future, so you may want to watch out for those books when they get released ☺

Conclusion

The rise of different work from home business ideas also gave rise to a lot of Amazon wannabe entrepreneurs. This means that the competition is now tougher than ever. A lot of new online entrepreneurs won't even be able to source a single product, but a part of those will be able to get their product to the Amazon marketplace. And that's where the battle begins. If you're in a place where you just launched your first product, then you must do everything in your power to become your own product evangelist. You must become your product's number one fan, at least in the beginning.

As you just discovered, there are 3 phases to increasing your Amazon sales. There's the optimization part where you deal with your listing – title, keywords, pricing, etc. Then there's the product part where you focus on improving your product as you gain more experience in your chosen market. Then the 3rd part, which is marketing your product for maximum sales. You don't necessarily have to treat it like steps 1 2 and 3. But I do recommend that you start with optimization and always be on the lookout for ways to improve your customer's buying experience.

Progress > Perfection

Before I let you go, I want to reiterate something that has been a huge part of my own Amazon mini-success story. And that is **progress is better than perfection.** Obviously, I'm not saying that you should just take random action and just keep breaking things. My point is that you should focus in applying the ideas inside this book as fast as possible while still doing them deliberately. 80% of the people who read this book will probably won't do anything with the information they gathered from it – the excuses will range from "it's too simple to work" or "it's too much work to bother," whatever your excuses are, I guarantee you that you won't make it in this business if all you do all day is complain about stuff that you have no control over. I'm sorry to be blunt and I'm sorry if I'm being mean to you right now, it's just that I've been writing these Amazon series for years now and I really hate seeing people fail when they could've easily done something about it.

My first book, "Amazon FBA for Beginners" is one of the most (if not the most) reviewed FBA book of all-time. I'm not saying that to brag. I'm saying that because I want you to know that because of the feedback I got from the reviewers, I am also heavily emotionally invested in the success of my readers. The reason why I keep writing these books is because I see how many lives can be changed if you just put your heart into something you think is important.

Go out there and produce quality products for your market, I guarantee you that that will be the best decision you'll ever make in your business.

Go prosper and see you on the other side,

Red

Review Request

If you like this book and it helped you in some way or another, I would like to request for you to kindly post a review on Amazon.com. Reviews are the lifeblood of every author out there and it helps in sharing the message.

I appreciate you and I look forward to hearing from you soon. Good luck on your business and I wish you all the success in the world.

Fulfillment by Amazon for Beginners

If you like to learn a simple and step by step way of getting started with Amazon FBA, I recommend that you check out my other books AMAZON FBA Step by Step (by Red Mikhail), FBA Product Research 101, Amazon Keyword Research 101, and FBA Product Sourcing Blueprint as well.

These are also available as audiobooks.

Just like this one, these 4 has a very simple language and conversational tone to it. If you found this book valuable, then you will like those 4 books as well.

OTHER BOOKS

I also have other books about making money online through different ways, check them out here:

Amazon's Associate Program

https://www.amazon.com/gp/product/B019EV4QA0/

One Hour Dropshipping System

https://www.amazon.com/gp/product/B014PU7S9Q

Amazon Product Listing Formula

https://www.amazon.com/gp/product/B0142ZWRC2

AMAZON FBA FUTURE UPDATES:

We're just scratching the surface. In the next few months (or years), I'm going to launch a series of books about:

FBA Advance Traffic & Marketing Strategies

Amazon Wholesaling

Amazon Retail Arbitrage

Amazon Dropshipping

And many more books related to starting and growing an Amazon ecommerce business.

If you want to make sure that you get a notification when these books go LIVE, just simply follow my Amazon author page here:

https://www.amazon.com/Red-Mikhail/e/B00X3KJ2TO/

(Click the follow button on that page to get instant updates from Amazon)

Million
Dollar
Ecommerce

A Beginner's Guide to Building
an Unforgettable Ecommerce Brand.
Pick a Profitable Idea, Start a New Online Business
and Scale It to a 7-Figure Income Source.

Red Mikhail

OTHER FBA BOOKS

AMAZON FBA Step by Step (by Red Mikhail) – to help you get started with Amazon FBA (the basics)

FBA Product Research 101 – an in depth guide to product research

Amazon Keyword Research 101 – an in depth guide to Amazon keyword research

FBA Product Sourcing Blueprint – a step by step blueprint on sourcing products and shipping it to Amazon/your preferred destination

Amazon FBA Sales Boost – 33 little tricks to triple your Amazon sales

These are also available as audiobooks.

You can find the whole series here:

https://www.amazon.com/gp/product/B086QZCJQQ

TABLE OF CONTENTS

Preface

Que Trailer... Insert *Honest Trailer from YouTube* voice guy here.

From the author that brought you the instant classic and the single most reviewed FBA book of all-time, Amazon FBA for Beginners, comes a new adventure that will take you through the process of creating a million-dollar brand. This is MILLION DOLLAR ECOMMERCE: A Beginner's Guide to Building an Unforgettable Ecommerce Brand.

Alright, sorry – I got carried away, enough of the hype.

Hey there, Red here and this is part 6 of the Amazon FBA series. Technically, this book isn't really solely about FBA or Amazon. It's about creating a successful ecommerce business from idea to execution by creating your own brand. The reason I'm putting it as part of the FBA series are 2 folds:

1 – This will reach more people interested in starting an ecommerce business. Since this series is getting hundreds of readers every day, it is likely that this will get some attention as well.

2 – I still recommend that most beginner ecommerce business owners (whether they create their own brand

or start with arbitrage) still sell their products first on Amazon.

And as always, the value of my books isn't really in the number of pages that it has. For me, it will always be about the actionable stuff. The truth is, I have no idea if this book will be 50 pages or 100 pages. Obviously, I have some sort of outline and estimate but I only use those as a guide and not as a "number of pages" goal. If you're the type of person whose focus is action and not just information, then I'm pretty confident that you'll love this one.
In addition, expect it to be super casual. This is just me talking to you in my living room, drinking beers, and just having a good time.

FOR BEGINNERS ONLY?

Although there will be some advance tactics and foundational stuff that ALL ecommerce business owners should learn, my primary target for this book is the beginner market.

If you're someone who already has a product line and someone who's already selling online for 3 years or more, then this book is not for you.

I try to cater to everybody and give as much info as I can but this book would serve you best if you're someone who's just getting started.

Introduction

If you think that it's too late now to start an e-commerce business, then you are greatly mistaken. The ecommerce industry is still growing and it will continue to grow for the years to come. This is probably one of the biggest (if not the biggest) opportunity of our lifetime. Millions of people will put (and are putting) themselves into a much better financial situation because of ecommerce. If you're reading this book and you're committed to taking action, then I see no reason why you won't be part of that movement.

Here are the best reasons why you should start an ecommerce business today:

#1 – It's Growing at a Break Neck Speed

It's crazy fast how ecommerce is growing. By starting your own business, you'll be able to ride the trend and you'll be able to build and grow a business faster than most people could ever imagined. And since *ecom* is a global business, you basically have the whole world as your potential market!

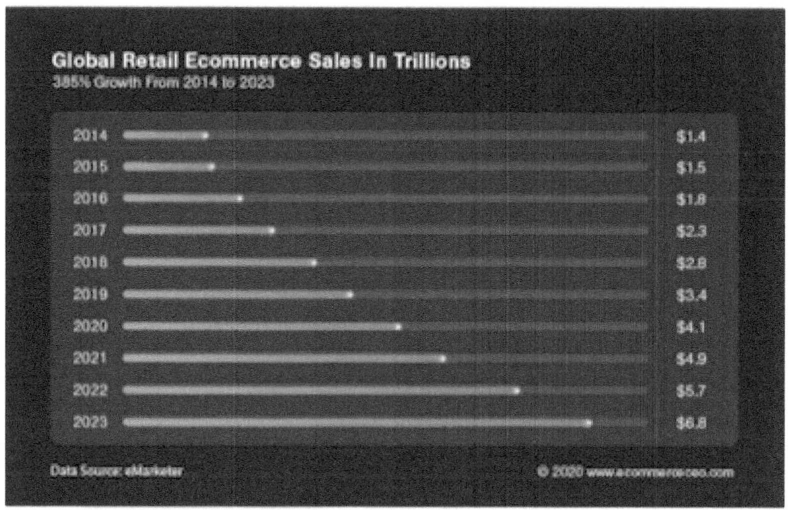

[Image 0.1]

#2 – Lots of New Niches to Target

There are literally hundreds if not thousands of potential niche markets to target. You don't have to rely on the niches that did well a few years ago. Today, you can make 7 figures even on niches that most people never heard of. There are new niches and new opportunities popping up every single day and you could be the one dominating that market.

The key is to create a product line that a market segment will buy over and over again.

#3 – Freedom Lifestyle

Because there's so much money to be made from ecommerce, it can help you live a financially comfortable life without sacrificing the things that you value most. The truth is, you can design your business in whatever size you like it to be. If you want to make 200k per year after tax and work 4 hours per day, then you can definitely do that. If you're more of a pure-bred entrepreneur and you enjoy the process of running a business, then you can spend as much time on your business as you want. One doesn't have to be better than the other. The point is you have a choice and building and running your own ecommerce brand allows you to have that choice.

1,000 FT. OVERVIEW

Allow me to give you an overview of how this whole ecommerce brand building process works.

Let me break it down chapter by chapter.

In **Chapter 1 – How to Create a Million Dollar Brand: Differentiate**, I will show you why you need to build your own brand and how to actually differentiate yourself from other sellers out there. You'll learn 4 different effective strategies on how you can stand out from the crowd and how to implement these to your own business. After this chapter, you'll see how big the opportunity is and you'll have a better understanding of the concept of branding and how it works in the ecommerce world.

In **Chapter 2 - How to Find Your Idea**, I'll show you how to find your niche or idea and then I'll show you how to come up with products that are more likely to have a demand and ready buyers at your fingertips. In this chapter, you'll learn how to rely less on tools and rely more on your "problem solving" skills to find the perfect idea for your new ecommerce business.

In **Chapter 3 - Product Sourcing Made Simple**, I will teach you exactly how to research potential manufacturers, evaluate suppliers, and source your products the right way. This is where most people get stuck, understandably, because this is the part where you invest money in the business. If you can get pass this part, then you'll already be head & shoulders against most people trying to start their own ecom brand.

In **Chapter 4 - How to Sell Your Physical Products**, I will teach you where and how to actually sell the products you sourced/created. I'll discuss the platforms you can use (i.e. Amazon/Shopify), the advantages and disadvantages of those platforms, and the best ways to drive traffic to your online store - both free and paid.

In **Chapter 5 - How to Scale Your Ecommerce Brand**, we'll discuss how to take your business to the next level. You'll learn the top 5 strategies most successful ecommerce brands do so you can create a 7-figure per year business. You'll learn stuff like *cart abandonment, AOV, time sensitive deals, upsells*, ads scaling, and other ecommerce strategies. By the end of this chapter, you'll have a buffet of actionable brand building and sales-getting strategies for you to build a 7-figure ecommerce brand.

THE REALISTIC MATH BEHIND A 7-FIGURE BUSINESS

Before you move on to chapter 1, I want to give you a *paint by the numbers* look at how you can create a 7-figure ecommerce brand.

If you're just starting out, it is very unlikely that your first and only product will make 7 figures per year. It can happen for sure, but that's just not a realistic expectation to set for yourself. Instead, I want you to focus on creating a product line up that complements each other. We will discuss more on this later but for now, let's focus on the numbers.

Let's say that the average price of the products you sell is $35. **If you want to gross 7 figures per year, then you have to sell at least 4 different products at $35 each and sell 20 pieces per product per day.**

Here's the math breakdown:

4 [Products] x 20 [Pieces Per Day] = 80 [Pieces Sold Per Day Sold]

80 [Pieces Per Day Sold] x $35 [Price in USD] = $2,800 Per Day

2,800 Per Day x 30 [Days] = $84,000 Per Month

$84,000 Per Month is basically 7-Figures Per Year

Now you might be thinking, damn, I can never sell 80 pieces of anything per day! That's too hard. Well, it is but it's not impossible. Remember, Amazon alone gets millions and millions of visitors per day and customers are buying billions worth of products per year. If you think about it hard enough, you'll see that selling 80 pieces per day of your products is a very realistic goal. Heck, you can do that just by selling on Amazon alone.

Imagine what would happen if you expand to creating your own store and actively advertise/market your own products? I'm telling you, it can get crazy awesome!

By looking at this simplified version of our business model, you'll now have a clearer understanding of how you can make this business work for you. Look at our sample numbers again, that number is possible for anyone and that someone could be you.

Let's do this!

Chapter 1
How to Create a Million Dollar Brand: Differentiate

First of all, let's define what a brand is and what it isn't. A brand is basically a business with the ability to roll out multiple products and make those products as successful if not more successful than the first one. A brand is an entity that separates you from the other "me too" products out there. What a brand isn't are logos, brand names, name in the building, or company videos - those are just part of the brand and they aren't the brand itself.

Why You Need to Be Different

There's a lot of good products out there and you need to stand out if you want to stay in business and thrive. **BEING DIFFERENT** is crucial because it allows you to say "Hey, I'm here – notice me!" without acting like a needy stalker. Having a brand automatically puts you in the category of the cool kids who gets noticed by almost everybody. Grateful Dead (the band) is still thriving today not because they're trying to be the best band ever. They don't care about that. By now, they already have an identity and a solid fan base whom they care about serving. Right now, they're just trying to be the best version of themselves. They're just trying to be the best version of who they already are. That doesn't mean they aren't evolving. I mean, for god's sake they hired John Mayer (a pop star! A far cry from their original front man Jerry Garcia) as their newest member since 2015. But the fan base accepted Mayer because, a.) he's actually really good in playing with the band **(in terms of ecommerce, he is a good complementary product),** and b.) he isn't the main attraction of the Grateful Dead, Mayer is only part of the bigger picture.

Whether you know the band or not, I do hope that you got the point I'm trying to say. It's not about being the best. It's not about not having any identity and being boring. It's not about being stale and never taking any risks. It's about being different and trying to evolve by giving the customers what they want and need.

So, with all these talk about differentiation, how do you actually do it? What are the practices that you can apply so you can differentiate your brand from the millions of products and businesses out there?

There are 4 MAIN WAYS I subscribe to when it comes to brand differentiation. Each of them is important and I make sure that I always apply ALL of them for my ecommerce brands.

THE CORE FOUR OF BRAND DIFFERENTIATION

#1 - Product Differentiation
#2 - Brand Look & Feel Differentiation
#3 - Marketing & Positioning Differentiation
#4 - Customer Service & Customer Experience
Differentiation

I'm sure there are other ways to differentiate but these are the core 4 that I follow. Feel free to research more on this if you want to. I do believe that these are enough for you to build a 7-figure ecommerce brand.

How to Build an Ecommerce Brand – Differentiation Strategies

#1 - Product Differentiation

This is bar none, the most important differentiation strategy of all. I would even claim that the other 3 doesn't work as well if you do not implement this one. I repeat: this is the most important way of building an ecom brand. Highlight that, write it down, put it on a note, and attach it to your fridge! By having a product that is actually different from the others, it will be much easier to build a business that will thrive in good times and in bad times. You can be different **by actually being different** - I know - what a concept, right? (LOL).

The key factor to remember when it comes to product differentiation is this: WHAT DO YOUR CUSTOMERS WANT AND NEED.

What They Want:

If you listen to your customers and you did your product research the right way, then you'll know exactly what they want when it comes to the product you are offering. For example, there's a segment of the "whey protein" buyers who doesn't like any sugar with what they're drinking. What can you do to solve this problem? What are the potential solutions for this issue? Well, you can put less sugar on your product. That's the most basic solution. But to make your offer more compelling, you can come up with possible substitute to sugar and put it on your whey protein brand instead. You can substitute sugar with neotame, aspartame, stevia or monk fruit. These are "artificial sweeteners" (but natural sugars) derived from extraction from various sources. Obviously, you still have to weigh the pros and cons before you put any of that stuff to your product. In this case, you're serving the market by removing what they want to be removed and adding a better substitute at the same time.

What They Need:

To serve the customers through your product, you also have to give them what they need. Sometimes, they don't even know what they need until you present it to them.

The most common customer needs are the following:

1 – Fair Price. All customers want a fair price for what they are buying. Don't get too greedy when it comes to profit and always offer fair market value for your products.

2 – Functionality. This is an obvious one. Your product has to be functional and it must be able to do what it promises to do.

3 – Effective/Efficient. Customers want a product that can give them the best and fastest result at the same time. *I.e. If you're selling a butcher knife, you better be damn sure that it can do its job fast and efficient. That means cutting should feel almost effortless.*

4 – Transparency. Make sure that you always mention the materials and ingredients your products are made of. This is especially true in consumable products, but important for any items nonetheless.

5 – Accessibility. Is your product available and easy to buy? You can put your products either on Amazon and your own website (or both).

6 – Options. Customers also need different options. Those options can either be about sizes, colors, types of ingredient, materials used, etc.

Note: In the next chapter, we will have a section called "How to Make Your Product Different" and we'll dive deep on the exact strategies to follow for product differentiation. I'll also give more examples so you'll have a clearer understanding of how this all works.

#2 - Brand Look & Feel Differentiation

This is what most people think about when they hear the word "brand." But as I've already told you, this is only part of the whole thing.
It is important to nail this one right at the very beginning since the way your brand's *look and feel* is going to be the foundation of how people perceived your brand.

Note: *This is especially true if you're selling outside Amazon.*

Here are the top 3 things to look at when it comes to your brand's look and feel.

#1 - Logo

Your logo is a combination of text and imagery. It acts as a visual representation of your company. It's the thing that represents your company virtually speaking. Since they can't see you (the founder) or any of your potential employees, your logo can act as the representative of your company. The logo also separates your brand to other peoples' brand in your niche.

Look at what your competitors' logo look like and try to be as different as possible.

Here are some of the best practices to remember when it comes to creating your logo:

- The color affects how people perceived your brand.
- Don't make the text too long.
- Have something easy to remember.
- Make the text as readable as possible.
- It should look timeless.
- Use less than 3 colors combined,
- Don't use any complicated new colors, just use any of the ones from the rainbow.
- Make sure that it'll work for variety of industries.

- Ensure that it looks good on black & white background which is going to be where most people will see your logo.
- Look at the logos of your competitors and try to be as different as possible (color and font text are great differentiators).

If you're just getting started, I recommend that you start with Fiverr for cheap logos but hire someone better as soon as you get your first few sales. *Re-invest your profits in your business and years from now, you'll be glad that you did that.*

#2 - Colors (Palettes)

Another factor that affects your brand's perceived value are the colors that you use in pretty much everything your company owns. You can use your choice of colors not only in your product/packages but also in your marketing materials, website, social media content, etc.

According to a few studies, the color affects more than 60% of buying decisions made by customers. Colors basically affect how they perceive your brand as a whole.

For example, blue emits tranquility, security, loyalty and trust. But it also emits coldness, fear, and masculinity. Yellow says bright, sunny, and energetic, but it also says unstable and irresponsible. There's no perfect color and it's not the only factor to look at for your ecommerce business, but it's an important one nonetheless.

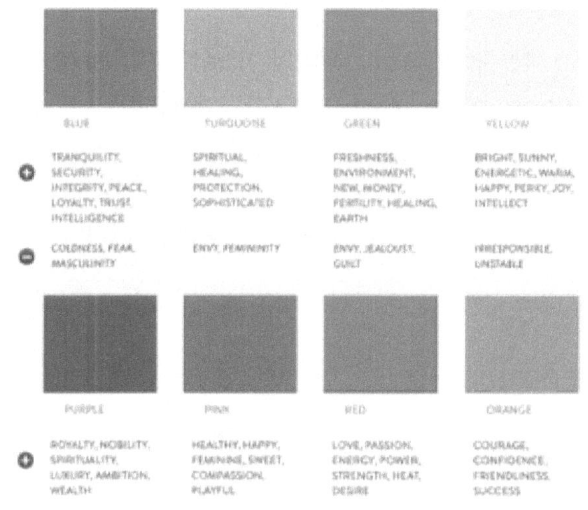

[Image 1.1]

Source: quicksrpout.com

HOW TO CHOOSE A CORE COLOR

It's honestly pretty simple: **"Know Your Target Demographic"**

Before you choose your top 2 to 3 dominating colors for your brand, the core colors you can use for your social media, websites, products, etc., make sure that you know WHO your customers are. *Are they mostly single people? Are they men or women? How old or how young are them?*

You need to choose your colors based on what they value or who they identify with.

If I'm selling to primarily men, then I'll probably choose between blue, red , black, and white (very neutral color).

If I'm selling to women (say beauty products), I'll most likely choose light pink, green, orange, or white.

These all depends as well on the product you are selling. But it has to match the energy that you want your product to emanate.

Quicksprout has a very detailed article about this and I recommend that you check it out here:

https://www.quicksprout.com/the-right-ecommerce-color-schemes/

#3 - Fonts

Honestly, I wouldn't worry about this too much in the beginning. The key is to start with safe and proven fonts to use.

Here are some fonts to choose for your ecommerce business and the corresponding niches that matches their perceived energy:

Montserrat (more industrial – electronic & industrial parts)

Crimson Text (skincare, yoga, spa, and other lifestyle products)

Oswald (for fitness, technology industry)

Overlock (for a little more playful look, clothes, baby products, and products serving the feminine side of things)

Playfair Display (dresses, beauty products, also feminine feel)

Remember to use the font of your choice in all your company assets. (advertising materials, marketing materials, website, sales pages, social media posts).

#3 - Marketing & Positioning Differentiation

People hate boring brands. Boring brands are dying and no one wants to be associated with them.

So how do we create a brand that's exciting and a brand that people love to talk about? How do we create what they call a "brand voice?" *Something that resonates with your target market and something that has a personality...*

Step 1 – Know who you're talking to

The first step is to know exactly who your target market is.

Here are some useful things to know about your target market:
A – Age Range
B – Gender
C – Nationality
D – Possible Political Leaning (Right, Left, Center)
E – Their Insecurities, Their Goals, What Product Similar to Yours They Are Currently Buying and What They Hate About These Products
(you'll learn how to research this in chapter 2)

Step 2 – Define who you want to be

Define who you are as a company. Are you fun and quirky? Are you serious and corporate like? I wouldn't say one is better than the other. But have some personality and let that personality define your business. In addition, that brand personality should match your audience. If you have younger buyers, then it makes sense to be a little playful with the language and tone you're using as a brand. If you have an older audience, then it's alright to be a little serious and straightforward.

At the same time, you have to know who you want to be as a brand.

Who are you as a company? What is your personality?

PERSONAL TO BUSINESS SPECTRUM

How personal do you want to be? How casual do you want to be perceived at?

I.e. Ryan Reynold's Gin Aviation.

Self-deprecating, funny, slightly laid back, feel good and feel awesome type of brand.

You can tell by their commercials that they appeal to a younger audience who doesn't like to take themselves seriously. And when I say younger, I say between 25-40.

Not all of us have the charisma of Ryan Reynolds and we don't necessarily have to have that anyway. We can still build a personality for our brand no matter who we are. We just have to commit to a certain attitude and know what we stand for as a company. Those Ryan Reynold Gin Aviation commercials work not because Ryan Reynolds is a big celebrity. It works because we know that Ryan Reynold is being an authentic (funny, charismatic, laid back) version of himself on those commercials – which is what we already know him for even before Aviation Gin.

EASY LANGUAGE TO INSIDER LANGUAGE SPECTRUM

Another thing to consider is the type of language you are using.

This will again all depend on your target market. How sophisticated are your buyers? Are you targeting the ones who are already in this market for a long-time? Or are you trying to convert new ones to join your market?

Here's an example I got from digitalmarketer.com (so credit to those guys!).

Bulletproof sells food and supplements for people looking to improve their health and lifestyles. Their founder Dave Asprey is well-versed in biohacking jargon—but you don't see a word of jargon in the emails to their subscribers.

Why? Because their customer avatar isn't an expert in the health space; they're an average person trying to figure out how to live a better lifestyle. That's why you'll see an easy language brand voice in Bulletproof's emails to their subscribers where they explain what refined carbohydrates are and why they're bad for you in easy-to-read language:

[Image 1.2]

Bulletproof doesn't use (or barely use) any of the insider language that "veterans" in this market use. They want to convert new people in their market so they have to use easy to understand language in their emails, website, and market materials so people would understand what they're trying to say.

How about your brand? Where does your business lie in the easy language to insider language spectrum? Only you can answer that.

#4 - Customer Service & Customer Experience Differentiation

CUSTOMER SERVICE

Nowadays, customer service is one of the main keys to long-term brand trust. Ironically, a lot of ecommerce brands today have terrible customer service so it won't be that hard to differentiate. By investing in customer service, you'll be above and beyond what customers expect. I dare you to call most of the companies you are patronizing right now, you'll probably go straight to a machine telling you how "you are important to us" while they make you wait for 2 hours only to be served by someone who can barely understand what you're saying. That's the kind of customer service that we're expecting nowadays. Our expectations are so low that we're not even expecting a reply on most of our customer service emails. All of these low expectation talk reminds me of this meme:

[Image 1.3]

Anyway, it's easy to solve this problem.

Invest in your customer service. There should be someone manning the emails from customers 24/7.

Yes, 24/7.

I know that this may eat up a bit of your profits in the beginning, but trust me, this is something that you have to do to build a brand that people love and trust.

Start with that then expand to having a phone number for customers to call. For now, a 24/7 customer email support is enough especially if you're just getting started.

CUSTOMER EXPERIENCE

There's a lot of ways to differentiate with customer experience. Here are the best ones I apply in all of my brands:

Easy Navigation – Your website should be clean and easy to navigate. Make your products easy to find in your website. In addition, they should be able to easily find customer support if they need it.

Packaging – People love a good unboxing experience. You can differentiate by having a premium feel for your products and making the box/packaging as appealing as possible. (i.e. Apple products)

Build Great Product Pages – Create product pages that are sleek and clean looking. It should show the product images, a few benefits of the product, and then a big add to cart/buy button.

Checkout Process – It bugs me that to this day, a lot of ecommerce stores I see are still using clunky and outdated checkout process. If I'm the customer, I should be able to know exactly what items I bought, how many I bought, and where to put my payment details. In addition, I should be able to look at the checkout process and trust that I'm not getting scammed. Add some trust badges on the page where they have to put their payment information.

Email Onboarding – Make your customers feel welcomed when they buy your product/s. Always send an order confirmation that shows the summary of their order plus the expected date of when it will arrive on their doorstep. In addition, try to be a little personal by adding some kind of thank you message or any informative message as well. For example, in your thank you email, you can send them additional information and link them to a blog (preferably your blog) about how to maximize what they just bought from your store. This adds value and shows that you care about your customers.

Faster Shipping and Easy Tracking – People are impatient nowadays. We just want to get what we ordered as fast as possible. Also, we want access to our order via easy tracking. If you can provide these 2, then you'll already be head & shoulders above your competition.

Optimize for Mobile – Make your website optimized for mobile. More than 50% of your traffic will come from smartphones so make sure that you do the following:

A – Make your website "responsive" (your designer will know what this is)
B – It should load really fast!
C – Don't use any pop-ups or any invasive ads
D – Reduce heavy content
E – Make your checkout process short and sweet. Guest checkout should be an option as well.

Differentiating your brand requires a lot of time, effort, and even financial investment in your part. But if you're serious in building an ecommerce brand that will last, then you have to do as much differentiation strategies as possible. Differentiating means trying your best to become the best option for your customers. All of these boils down to serving the customers with the best of your ability. The more you differentiate, the more value you bring to your buyers who then turns into loyal customers.

In the next chapter, we'll talk about how to find your niche/idea and then we'll discuss the exact strategies to use for producing a product that people love and recommend to other people.

Chapter 2
How to Find Your Idea

Most beginners looking for their first niche or product idea start their research with products. They buy software tools and join online courses hoping they would get that "little nugget" of information that will lead them to their perfect first product. STOP. This doesn't work and this type of mindset will only lead you to failure.

Look for problems instead of products.

This is, quite frankly, what we are all doing in this business. We're just trying to solve someone's problem. We can tackle this in two ways.

Either solve a small problem that millions of people have, or solve a big problem that thousands of people have. So you can either focus on SCALE or MAGNITUDE. Truth be told, one is not better than the other.

You can sell lots of stuff and make millions or you can sell a decent amount of stuff and still make millions – it's just a matter of scale and the impact you are having in the market. Also, you don't necessarily have to choose one over the other to make money with ecommerce. The only key is to find a problem and solve it.

4 WAYS TO FIND PROFITABLE NICHE IDEAS

#1 - Self-Search/Products You're Already Using

I always start by looking within myself and finding problems that I am experiencing or something I experienced in the past.

Are there some products that you hope are available but aren't? Are you not satisfied with the products you are currently using? *Your facial wash? Your body bar? How about your shampoo?* Someone somewhere out there is complaining about something about a certain product. That someone could be you. You can turn this into an opportunity by creating a much better solution to the problem you are currently experiencing with the products you are using right now.

What are the problems that I am currently experiencing in my life?

What are the complaints that I have with the products that I am currently using?

Always listen to the type of language you are using on a daily basis.

For example, in the past few weeks, I've been having trouble with the following:

1 – Back Pain (oh God, every day is a struggle)
2 – Sleeping Consistency (zombie mode!)
3 – Having New Braces and Having a Hard Time Flossing
4 – Canker Sore (these little bastards hurt!)

These are all opportunities that can lead to a great product. These are all problems that I can solve for myself.

What are the products that are currently working for me but could be improved upon? What products do I currently use but aren't really working for me?

We're not trying to re-invent the wheel here and we're not exactly trying to go to Mars. All of our daily problems are also possibly something that other people are experiencing. Those are opportunities in disguise and they are problems we can solve for other people.

#2 - Amazon Market Gap

One of the best ways to find a niche idea that already has a proven market is via what I call "Amazon Market Gap Research"

It's basically the art of looking at well reviewed products on Amazon and then finding gaps in the market by reading the negative feedback that the customers left on Amazon.

I'm telling you right now, you DO NOT need to pay thousands of dollars for product research tools, and approaching research this way is going to be more beneficial for you long-term speaking.

In my book *Product Research 101*, I argued that product research tools should only be complementary tools instead of the main way to find products. And quite honestly, I think I changed a lot of minds with my approach.

So here's the skinny of how I do my Amazon research.

Step 1 - Look for products that already exist

By now, you should already have some kind of idea of what niche you want to be in. If not. I recommend that you go back to the first niche research idea. As an alternative, you can also look at the Amazon best-seller list. I recommend that you start with categories like:

A – Toys & Games
B – Beauty & Personal Care
C – Handmade Products

D – Home & Kitchen
E – Kitchen & Dining
F – Patio, Lawn & Garden
G – Sports & Outdoors
H – Tools & Home Improvement

I do not recommend starting with computers, electronics, camera, cell phones, or pretty much anything with some kind of electronic part to operate. (I would say small battery operated ones is an exception.) Most of these products are super expensive to source and could easily break which can cost you hundreds of thousands of dollars.

I'm not saying you shouldn't be in those niches EVER, I just recommend that you start outside those categories first so you can avoid losing money that you probably don't even have yet. I'm just being realistic here because I don't want you to quit this business in your first year.

Step 2 – Once you found a product, start reading ALL the negative reviews and make a list of their complaints.

For example, I found this product called LED Light Arm Band under the Reflective Gear sub-category.

[Image 2.1]

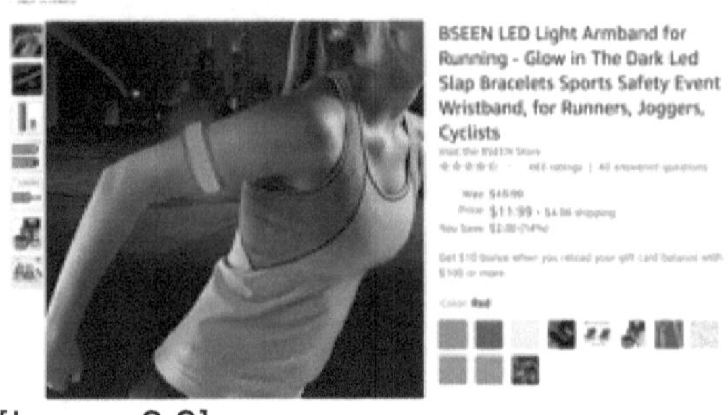

[Image 2.2]

This seems like an interesting product that solves a big problem for a lot of runners, which is getting seen and being visible in the dark.

So I dive deeper into the product and read some negative reviews.

By reading the 1-3 star reviews, I found out that the product issues are the following:

1 – The size is either too big for some women and too small for some men   [this seems to be number one concern]
2 – Hard to install and remove battery
3 – It's not that bright

After you found these issues, your job is to create a solution that will solve these problems for them. And that's basically how you create a better product that customers already want.

1 – Find a product that is already selling well
2 – Find the issues and concerns or the current market gaps
3 – Create a product that solves these issues

Just do this process over and over again and you'll have a variety of profitable niches to possibly be in.

A Note on **Value Skewing** (which we'll discuss a bit more on the latter part of this chapter):

I probably mention this technique in all of my books so I'm sorry if I have to repeat this over and over again (but it's that important). Once you found the things that you can improve upon, you have to choose the issues/concerns that your market values the most. You cannot possibly solve all of their problems but you can focus on the ones that are the most important to them. The more they complain about it, the more important it is to them that you solve that issue.

#3 - Google Trend Search

Using Google Trend is a good way to gauge the market's current demand or interest for a certain topic. *You obviously shouldn't limit your research with this tool as it only serves as an additional metric to evaluate the demand for the niche you are targeting.*

You can go to this link and log in using your Gmail account:

https://trends.google.com/trends/

When you use this tool, I recommend that you start with keywords directly related to the product that you want to sell.

Here are some examples:

1 – Product Based Keywords:

Fishing rods – this is a product name or a niche idea so I'll try to look at the 5-year data as well as the recent 12 months.

I like seeing graphs that looks more a bit like these:

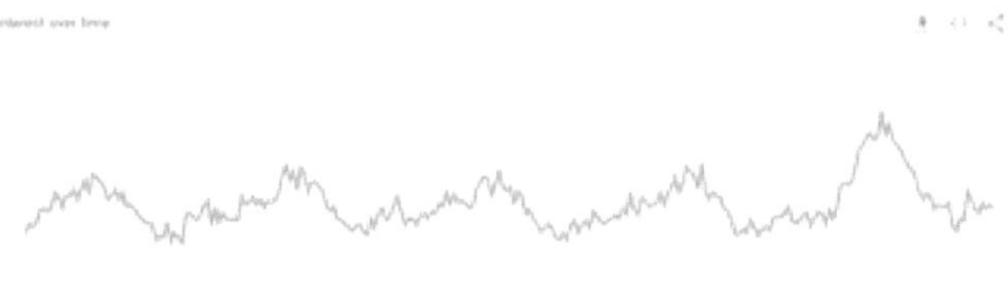

[Image 2.3]

[Image 2.4]

It doesn't go too up and down and it has a consistent number of searches.

Now that doesn't mean that it shouldn't have any peaks and lows, that's pretty normal…

For example, for the keyword "Electric toothbrush" [image 2.5], you will see in the 5 year graph below that there are some peaks and valleys especially during the last 3rd or 4th week of November.

But if you look at the graph as a whole, you will see that it's growing at a consistent 5% every year. Not exactly the hottest niche to be around but it's a consistent one nonetheless.

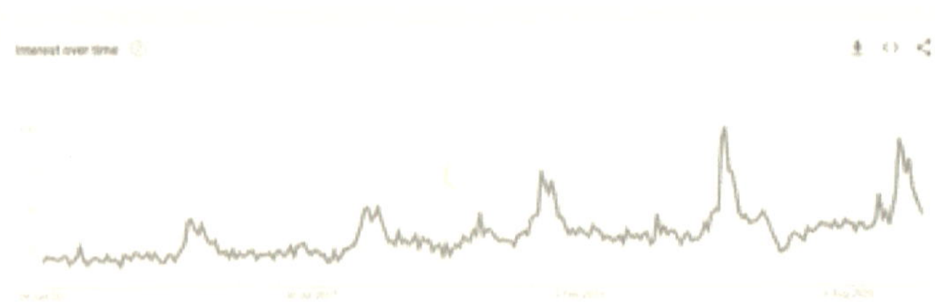

[Image 2.5]

2 – Problem/Solution Based Keywords:

I also like to look at keywords that mentions a problem or some kind of intention to find a solution.

For example, "Back pain massage"

[Image 2.6]

So how do we evaluate these results?

Personally, I like to see trends that are either going up consistently for the last 5 years and/or something that isn't too cyclical or seasonal in nature.

I also like to target products that are timeless by nature. *For example, a back pain chair massage would probably still be useful in 2040. Humans have been experiencing back pain since the beginning of time and it's a problem that likely won't go away anytime soon. Fishing rods would always be in demand because humans will always feel the need to fish even just as a sport or a family outdoor activity. We can't help but do it because billions of our ancestors did it before us.*

The worst type of trends are fads like "fidget spinners." I would usually avoid going into markets that shows *wayyyyy* too much growth in such a limited amount of time (months, even days but not years). I would rather choose slow but consistent growth because there's higher likelihood that it will still be here to stay for a very long time. It's great to look at trends and ride that wave but be careful and use your best judgement because there's a good chance that you're only riding a fad.

#4 - Other People's Complaints

One of my favorite ways to find opportunities is by simply keeping my ears open for complaints. While other people shy away from hearing complaints, I'm always (at least in the back of my mind) open to hearing them.

We often hear people say things like:

This sucks…
I hate this…
I wish I could…
I wish there was…
Can this be any faster?
Why isn't there a…
I hate product X
I'd love to _____

All of these complaints are an opportunity to solve a problem. These are opportunities to create great products that are more likely to sell because they are solutions to common complaints.

This sucks… What sucks? Can you help this guy remove suckage?

I hate this… What do you hate? Can we make this better for you?

I wish I could… I wish there was a______ You wish you could what? Can you make a product that makes this wish possible?

Can this be any faster?... Can you make whatever this is, faster?

Why isn't there a... a what? Can we create this for you?

I hate product X... What do you hate about product x? Can we make a better one?

I'd love to have a _____ that does ________ .... What do you want and what does it do? I'd love to make this for you.

Always be on the lookout for these complaints and you'll be able to build a mind that is open to new opportunities. Have the mindset of a value creator and problem solver – that's how you come up with product ideas that sells.

How to Make Products Great Again

In a world full of instant, copy cats and shortcuts, I want you think about how you can be original. How can you solve the customers' problems and create value for other people?

This all revolves around the technique called **VALUE SKEWING**. It's about tailoring your products based on what the customers value. It's about skewing value out of things that your audience think are important.

Now, being original doesn't mean inventing a completely new product. It's more about figuring out what you can improve upon an existing product so you can serve the market better than everybody else.

If you followed my suggestions in chapter 1, then you'll know exactly which values you can skew to make a certain product better.

Here are the things to consider when you're value skewing:

#1 - Design

People love a better designed product. It makes them feel good using the product and it affects how we perceive a product's value. Look at what your competitors are doing and ask yourself, "Is there a way I can make this look and function better?"

Ask your supplier if they can create a better design for you. This again comes back to your research. What do the customers want and need? Give it to em' and watch the avalanche of sales come in.

#2 – Functions and Features

Is there anything it could do better?
Something it could do that it couldn't before?

Are there any new features you can add that your customers will appreciate?

In the world of motorcycles, ABS brakes used to be reserved only for big bikes and premium motorcycles. But today, ABS technology is slowly becoming a legal requirement to sell small or big bikes in some countries. It's because this feature, or this function of having ABS brakes has been proven to save lives and avoid accidents.

Look at your own product and find out what features it could have that will make your customers' lives easier and better. It doesn't even have to be some kind of new technology. For example, a simple change in *grippable* material for an electric shaver can alter the way the customer uses the product. Remember this: just one change in feature can elevate your product compared to the rest of your competition.

#3 - Price

If you're selling on Amazon, it wants your product to be as cheap as possible. Remember Amazon's motto, "the lowest price possible with the widest selection." Lower your price as much as possible.

If you're selling outside Amazon (on your own website), I still highly recommend that you go as low as your margins could allow. In the long-term, having an affordable and better offering is still the best business practice because it gives the customers' more value for their money.

#4 - Materials or Ingredients

In chapter 1, we talk about using different materials or ingredients that people love to see on the products they are buying.

For example, you can use ALL ORGANIC ingredients so you can add value to a market that demands that type of product. You can assure them by having a product that is 100% plant based, gluten free, vegan, dairy free, and soy free. Each one of these are one value being skewed in stack of another. So it all comes down to knowing your market. *What ingredients or materials do they want in their product? What ingredients do they want to avoid? The more value you skew in their favor, the more likely they are to patronize your product.*

Another part is adding ingredients that solves a specific problem.

Here are some examples:

Tranexamic Acid & Kojic Acid – Lightens Skin (a very good value stack for the Asian market who wants to have lighter skin)

Rhodiola – Reduces Stress (great for products that promises renewed energy and less stress)

Cranberry – Antioxidants, vitamins, and minerals (great for products that promises improvement in immunity and urinary health)

Look at the last few products you bought, especially the consumable ones (food, vitamins, skin care). They probably not only listed their ingredients but also mention the benefits of each one of them.

Applying the concept of Value Stacking is probably the best way to get new customers and retain them for the long-term. The key here is to add materials or ingredients that you can attach to a specific benefit.

The more value you stack in their favor, the more likely they are to convert as customers.

#5 – Customer Service

Ah, the forgotten art of good customer service. In today's business climate, a good customer service is now part of the product. I recommend investing in a full-time customer service representative either by email or by phone. It's a worthy investment and something that will serve your brand well.

#6 – Customer Experience

Another way to add value to your customers is by improving the buying experience.

Here are some best practices to follow:

1 – Make your website simple and easy navigate

2 – Make the colors easy to look at

3 – Give the benefits and features of the products

4 – Clear instructions on how to pay

5 – Offers fast shipping

6 – Easy to locate customer service, plus wider choices of communication (email, chat, and call)

7 – Shows product reviews below the product pages (SUPAH CRUCIAL!)

I recommend that you checkout ORGANIFISHOP since this is a really good example of a well-run ecommerce business. I have no affiliation with this company, I just really like the way they run their e-commerce business.

https://www.organifishop.com/

#7 - Main Benefits

Another value to stack is the main use or benefits of the product.

Can it solve a more painful (or at least a different) problem?

For example, the pillow was invented so that insects would not crawl on human's faces whenever we sleep. At some point, some smart dude pointed out the obvious and said "This sleeping on a piece of rock thing sucks." Then some smarter dude started using softer materials and here we are in the 21st century, spoiled in our cushy pillows. Thanks random smart dude or dudette!

The original recipe for Coca-Cola was actually used as cure for morphine addiction. There's a long history there but today we just drink it for our sugar addiction and it's legal too! Hooray, I guess.

My point is, try to find other uses for products that already exist. This is obviously a hard exercise to do but a good one nonetheless. It helps you transform your mind and it creates a shift in the way you think. By doing this exercise often, you start to become a value-creator instead of a copy-cat.

Chapter 3
Product Sourcing Made Simple

Your suppliers are the literal lifeblood of your product inventory. They're the ones who manufactures your product for you and they have control over whether you'll have something to sell or not.

In this chapter I want to show you the following:

a – Where and how to find the best suppliers for your product.
b - How to evaluate whether you should hire them or not.
c - How to make your first order so you can make the process as seamless as possible.

Where and How to Find Suppliers

#1 – Start Local or Focus on Product-Place Specialty

If it's possible and if it make sense financially speaking, then I highly recommend that you start local. And by local, I mean your city or state. If you're going to sell primarily in the U.S., that **Made in the U.S.A** badge will always have a big effect on how people perceive your product. If you think about it, where your product is made from is a "value stack" in itself. People still value the country, state, or place where the product is made from.

Start with Google Search

Pretty obvious advice but it works. Search for your product name + add the state, city, or county you live in. There may be some potential suppliers for your product in your local area. This makes the shipping cheaper and the communication easier for both parties.
Some example searches are:
Product Name + Private Label + State
Product Name + Private Label + County
Product Name + Private Label + Country
Product Name + Manufacturer + State
Product Name + Manufacturer + County
Product Name + Manufacturer + Country
Product Name + Supplier + State
Product Name + Supplier + County
Product Name + Supplier+ Country

Another thing to consider is the **Product-Place Specialty.**

Most of the time, a certain line of products are going to be manufactured in one concentrated place.

For example, if you want your own private labeled brand of whiskey, then you will most likely find most of the manufacturers in Tennessee.

In this case, you can start your search with keywords like:

Private label whiskey Tennessee
Whiskey distiller Tennessee

Obviously there are other states that you can also search for, but I recommend that you start with the place with the most concentrated manufacturer of whatever product you want to sell.

If you look at the data from stacker, https://stacker.com/stories/2571/top-industries-every-state, you'll see the top industries in every state and that would be a good indicator of potential product availability and affordability for whatever niche you are in.

In other cases, you will have to expand beyond your local state and go international. That doesn't mean that you have to choose China immediately. You still have to think about product-place specialty and see what country will produce the best product for you.

Remember, it's not just about the "Made in USA" badge of honor. Other countries also have their specialties too and that could also act as a value stack that your customers will value. *I.e. "Made in Italy" – cars, motorcycles, anything fashion related, "Made in the Philippines" – coconut products, delicacies, unusual desserts, "Made in Japan" – literally anything industrial that is of the highest quality and something that will still work until all of us die from climate change. Stereotypes has some value after all.*

#2 – Alibaba.com

This is the most common way to find Chinese suppliers and this is where most people get started, and that's for a good reason. There's millions of products here and most sellers can understand and speak decent English.
In addition, there's also Trade Assurance in Alibaba so you're safer in terms of not getting scammed and ghosted.

To search for a product, just simply type your product name on the search bar.

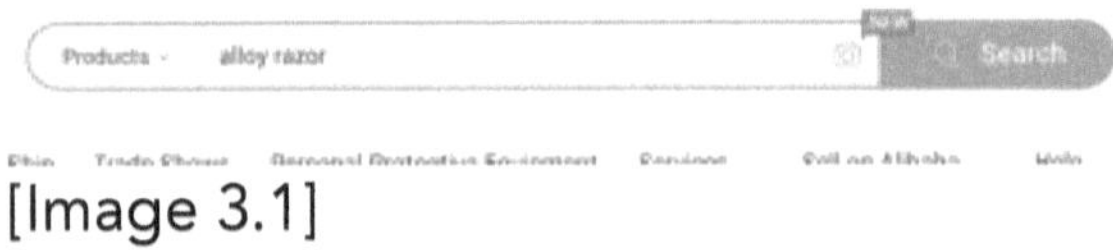

[Image 3.1]

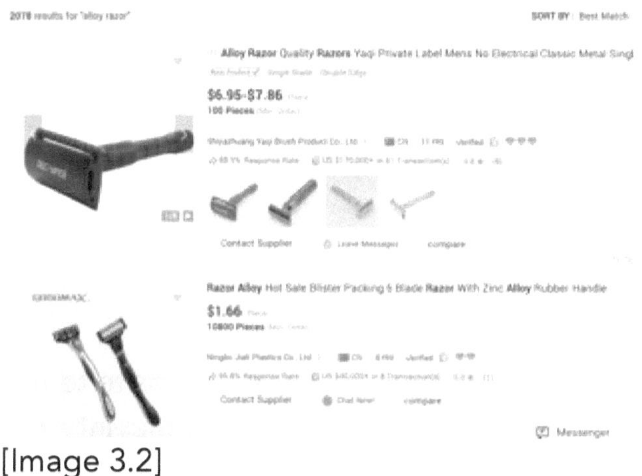

[Image 3.2]

There will always be a variety of style and colors to choose from so look for the design that you want for your own product. Also, don't hesitate to ask a supplier if they can change some things (either function or design) to fit your own vision of the product.

Here's a few advice if you choose to go this route:

a – Make sure that you're dealing directly with the manufacturer and not a broker so you can save money
b – Always read up on the company profile and check their website as well to see if they are legit
c – Always be polite in approaching their customer service
d – Be aware of their office hours if you want faster replies
e – Be patient because English isn't their first language

f – Don't ask stupid questions like "can I get a discount" on your first message.

Later in the chapter I'll show you how to evaluate your suppliers.

#3 – 1688.com

Here's another one of my new favorite website to use that is rarely discussed by those big time internet marketing gurus.
The process for research is pretty much the same as Alibaba and other platforms, so I'm just going to give you some of the best practices to follow if you use this platform.

A – Using 1688 requires an app called WeChat. It's like their WhatsApp over in China and it gives you direct communication with the manufacturer.

B – They mostly speak in Mandarin so use the WeChat app to translate whatever you want to ask them.

C – Use an extension called "Google Translate" on the Google Chrome store since the 1688 website is in Chinese.

D – The price that you will see on the product pages are already possibly the lowest they can give. Unlike Alibaba, the price on 1688 is mostly fixed because most (if not all) sellers here are wholesalers and direct manufacturers. Nonetheless, you can still negotiate with them especially if you're going to order more units.

E – The prices you see on 1688 are in RMB(CNY) so you need to have your currency converter handy. I just use the one provided by Google.

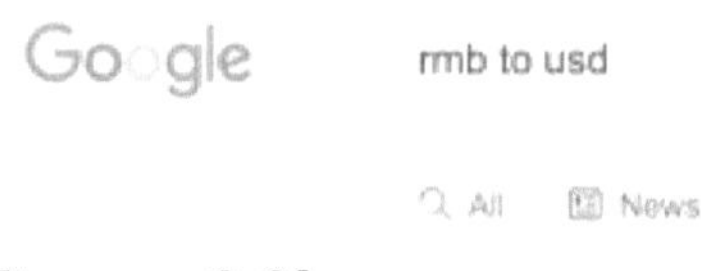

[Image 3.3]

You can also find free currency converter apps on the Apple or Android App Stores.

#4 – Make It Yourself

If you lack the capital and you have a lot of time, then why not learn to make the product yourself? This may not be possible for some people but
a lot of ecommerce businesses actually started this way.

If you make the product yourself, then it's going to be much cheaper to produce and ship since you have full control over the whole thing. In addition, you'll have higher profit margins and you'll make more money with a lot less capital investment.

Here are some ways to help you get started:

1 - Hire an Expert as a Consultant

If you really have no idea how to create the product and you're clueless about everything you need, then start with hiring an expert to teach you how to make it. Most experts will gladly work on a per hour basis as a consultant and you can just ask anything you want in that time.

2 - Hire an Expert to Create It with/or for You

Too lazy to learn everything by yourself? Then partner with an expert to create it with or for you. Most experts who can create products are notoriously bad marketers and entrepreneurs. Sure, they could be really good with the product creation part but most couldn't sell their way out of a paper bag even if their life depends on it. This is where you come in. You can be the Steve Jobs to their Steve Wozniak.

3 - Learn from Paid Online Courses or Free YouTube Videos

If you have almost zero budget, I recommend that you start with cheap online courses or free YouTube videos. You can pretty much learn everything on YouTube nowadays and there's just no excuse anymore not to get started.

EVALUATING YOUR SUPPLIERS

So how do you know which suppliers to work with? How do you make sure that you pick the right manufacturer for your awesome product?

That's where we use our 9-point criteria.

The more criteria we hit, the more likely we are to hire a specific supplier.

#1 – Direct Supplier/Manufacturer

Only work with direct suppliers or manufacturers who creates their own product. There's a lot of middle-man out there and they will naturally increase the price you pay per unit.

To avoid the middle-man, I always look at their company profile and even ask them directly if they are indeed the manufacturer and not just another company who will pass the work to other suppliers.

#2 – The price makes sense and you'll still make money selling the product

There's a lot of factors that will significantly affect your profit margin. Stuff like weight of the product, the packaging, and shipping options. This will obviously be different for every product, but as a general rule, I like to follow the 5X RULE. If you've read some of my books, then you probably already heard of this. In fact, I mention this in every single book I write and will continue to do so because it has serve me and thousands of my readers well.

The 5X RULE states that you should **sell your product for at least 5X the cost per unit to achieve breakeven point.**

That means if you want to be on the safe side, you should be able to sell a product on Amazon or your own website for at least 5x what it cost you to produce/source it.

For example, if your cost per unit is $5, then you should be able to see similar products on Amazon and other platforms that sells for at least $25.

The reason we want to follow the 5x rule as a general rule is because we won't necessarily know every single detail of our expenses until we're actually selling the product. There's just too many potential unexpected expenses that may creep up so we better bet on the safe side.

I recommend a tool called FBA Calculator if you want to go in-depth on expenses, Amazon fees, etc.

Here's the link for a free download:

https://junglescout.grsm.io/fbacalculator

#3 – You can actually afford the Minimum Order Quantity (MOQ)

Not all of us has an extra 5 million bucks just lying around the house, so we better make sure that we can actually afford to invest the necessary MOQ to produce the product.

Ask yourself, *what can I realistically afford to invest right now?*

#4 – Product and sample quality is up to par to your standards

Make sure that you order a sample and double check the quality of the product. Try its functions and see if it delivers on what it promises to do. If you're not thrilled about your own product, then chances are other people won't be as well.

#5 – Acceptable LEAD TIME [Manufacturing Lead Time]

Make sure that you agreed upon a specific time-frame of completion and shipping date. This is called lead-time. This is the amount of time they need to manufacture and package the product for it to be ready for shipping. If you're ordering from Alibaba or 1688, lead-time doesn't usually include the shipping time. This is something that you have to ask your suppliers since there are many types of lead-time and the definition may change depending on who you're talking to.

#6 – Clear Communication

The language barrier may play a part in this, but in general, I like to work with suppliers that replies fast and clearly. That means they should be able to answer my questions with clarity and I should be comfortable in asking them any questions related to my order. Not answering the questions and avoiding minute but important details is a big sign that you shouldn't work with a certain supplier.

#7 - Years in Business.

I usually only work with manufacturers who has been in the business for at least 5 years. There's going to be less risk of default and they already know the ins and out of manufacturing, shipping, and all that crazy stuff that us ecommerce business owners have to go through. A good manufacturer can act as a "quasi mentor" because of their experience. We just have to ask questions about things that we don't understand.

For example, when I was just getting started, I used to ask dozens of questions about the shipping process and they gladly responded to my questions in detail because I am a customer. This is how I was able to learn the shipping process fairly early in the game which I suspect has saved me thousands of dollars over the years.

#8 – Product Specs Change

Can they create new product mold? Can they change some aspects of the product to match your preferred specification, design, and features?
The more changes they can accommodate, the better.

#9 – You trust them (intuition)

You did your research, the numbers make sense, and the supplier check all the boxes. Now it's time to ask yourself: DO I TRUST THEM? Do you actually have a good feeling about this supplier. My intuition has played a big part in my e-commerce journey and the more I follow it, the more I seem to achieve success in my business.

MAKING YOUR FIRST ORDER

Now it's time to make your first order. If you did your research and you follow the criteria that I just showed you, then making you first order should be a breeze.

Step 1 - Negotiate the MOQ

First you have to ask yourself what you can realistically afford.

Be respectful in asking for any discounts and don't negotiate on the first message you sent. Try to build a relationship first and ask important questions related to the product so they'll know that you mean serious business.

Just know that if you are ordering from China and you're working with a direct supplier, then *they are most likely already providing you the lowest possible price*. Competition in China is fierce and these companies want to work with you in the long-term. They want to win your business and providing the lowest price possible is one of the keys for them to achieve that.

Step 2 - Make sure that the number works

Follow my 5x rule for this.

Step 3 - Get clear on the shipping

Make sure that you know who pays what. There's lots of type of shipping like: ex works, freight on board, and delivery duty paid.

Ex Works is when the seller is only responsible for making the product available to a specific designation (usually a port) and the buyer becomes responsible for everything else.

Freight on Board (FOB) is when the seller is responsible for shipping to the port (usually your country's port) and then you have to hire freight forwarders to ship it to your designated location.

There's many types of FOB so make sure to read up on it here:

https://corporatefinanceinstitute.com/resources/knowledge/other/freight-on-board-fob/

Delivery Duty Paid is when the seller is responsible for everything till the product arrives at your preferred designation.

My advice: Research on the pros and cons of these options then slowly realize that Delivery Duty Paid is the best! Seriously though, if you're a beginner DDP is definitely the best option because you don't have to worry about anything else except making sure that the product sells.

Then there's the shipping method of either Air or Sea.

I can write a whole book about shipping (I actually did) so I'm just going to explain the skinny here:

1 - You have two main options if you're sourcing outside the U.S. It's either AIR OR SEA.

Air is going to be faster (usually 3-10 days) but it is more expensive.

Sea is going to be much cheaper (2x-3x cheaper than air) but it can take 30-45 days before it arrives to your preferred designation.

ADVICE: MIX THE TWO!

This allows you to learn both the shipping process for air and sea and it saves money as well since you're doing the other half via sea.

Note: Check out part 4 of this FBA series called FBA Product Sourcing Blueprint to get a whole step by step instruction on how to deal with shipping.

Chapter 4
How to Sell Your Physical Products

Start with Amazon FBA

I will tell you straight up that you should start with Amazon FBA because of these 2 things:

1 - Free Traffic

Amazon gets millions of visitors per day and a lot of them are already looking for the type of product you are selling. All you have to do is leverage Amazon's search engine and optimize your listing for the keywords you are targeting. With Amazon, you already have an existing audience that you know are ready to buy your product. If you did the value-skewing part of this training, then I have no doubt that you'll create a much better product compared to your competition.

2 – Paid Market Test

Even if you're not 100% sure that your product will sell like gangbusters, with Amazon, you'll also know if people are actually interested in purchasing your product. Even if you're spending money on Amazon Ads, you don't necessarily have to go broke to test things out. With Amazon, there's less risk of ordering inventories and not selling it because there's millions of potential customers who can see your listing.

Think of it as a paid market test. Whenever you're selling a new product, you're basically trying to test a hypothesis and you're trying to find out the truth. In this case, the hypothesis will always be "Is my product going to sell?"

You'll never really know until you test it and actually start selling your product online. The best place for you to do that is through Amazon FBA.

Signing-Up on Amazon

You can register for an account here:

https://sellercentral.amazon.com/

1 – You can start as an individual seller for free + fees

Or

2 – You can choose to become a professional seller for $39.99 a month

I recommend the second one since you're here to sell lots of stuff and not just flip items you found on eBay.

KEYS TO A SUCCESSFUL AMAZON BASED PRODUCT

#1 – Have a Damn Good Product

Just simply apply the lessons you learned in the past few chapters and I'll have no doubt that you'll create a superior product in comparison to your competition.

#2 – Keywords are Crucial

If you want to sell lots of stuff on Amazon, then you gotta target the right keywords that are highly related to your product. Most people think that long-tail keywords (3-4 terms, low searched) is the key to making money because they can easily ranked for it on Amazon. The truth is, it's all about the main/competitive keywords. It's all about the keywords that are getting thousands and thousands of searches. The good news is you don't need to have any of those paid keyword research tool to get started. You can simply use your common sense and look at what keywords your competition are using. Usually, you'll find these main keywords on the product title.

For example, if your product is a "car seat cover for dogs", then you can just type that term on Amazon and look at what the competition is doing.

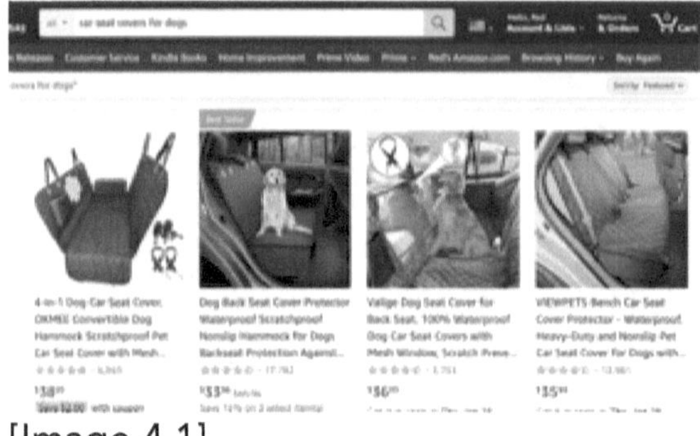

[Image 4.1]

Just by doing this research, I found out that my competitors are targeting the following keywords:

Waterproof
Scratchproof
Backseat Protection
Scratch Prevention
Cover Protector
Durable
Non-slip
Car Seat Cover for Dogs

You can then use these keywords for your title, Amazon keywords meta data, and other parts of your listing.

There's more strategies you can apply for keyword research but this is the most basic and easiest one to implement.

#3 – Creating a Highly Optimized Product Listing

Your listing acts as a 24/7 salesman for your product. He's your hype man. He's your #1 digital supporter and he will always only be as good the salesman that you made him to be.

You are responsible for putting your product in as good a light as possible and you can do that via your listing.

Here are the most important part of an Amazon listing:

A – Title. Always use your main keywords on your title but DO NOT overoptimized and just randomly mention the terms.

Here's a simple formula that works for me:

Brand Name + Primary Keywords + Main Features

1 – Start with your brand name.

2 – Choose the top 2-3 terms to put on your title as primary keywords. Make sure that they are relevant.

3 – Then add the most important features your customers need to know.

Example:

Ortho-Max | Biodegradable Bamboo Toothbrush | Eco Friendly, Soft Nylon Bristles, Organic Material, Smooth Handle, 100% Recyclable.

Quick tip: Make sure that you use a vertical bar to separate the 3 parts.

B – Bullet Points. Here's a simple formula for bullet points.

Line #1 - Feature + Benefits

I give them the biggest and most important feature that they are looking for and I explain how this affects them.

Line #2 - Feature + Benefits

I give them the 2nd biggest feature that they are looking for and I explain how this affects them.

Line #3 – Differentiate

I try to differentiate my product through a specific feature or benefit.

Line #4 - Twist the Knife + Solve the Problem

I give them a big problem and then I explain to them how my product solves this problem.

Line #5 - Guarantees
I give them some sort of guarantee that the product works or else they can send it back to me and get a 100% refund.

C – Images. Always use high quality images shot by professional photographers who specialize in physical products.

***

To get more info on keyword research and setting up your listing, I recommend the following resources:

https://www.wordstream.com/blog/ws/2018/10/23/amazon-keyword-research

https://blog.repricer.com/resources/complete-guide-amazon-keyword-research/

https://www.plytix.com/blog/amazon-keyword-research-for-brands

https://manychat.com/blog/amazon-listing-optimization/

https://www.repricerexpress.com/optimise-your-amazon-product-listings/

Surprise, surprise – my book! **Amazon Keyword Research 101** where I discussed how to find the best keywords without using any tool at all and how to create an effective product listing from start to finish.

***

How to Get Amazon Reviews

If you want more organic sales for your product, then you gotta have reviews that can act as your social proof. Customers love to buy products that other people are already using.

So how do you get consistent product reviews especially if you're just getting started

#1 - Lower your prices

In the beginning, you might want to consider lowering the prices to the point that you're only breaking even. This will get you more sales which means more people trying out your product. This is definitely a short-term sacrifice that will yield you great results in the future. Not everybody has the guts to do this because, quite honestly, it sucks not making a profit from your hard work. But if you choose to do this now, I have a feeling that you'll thank yourself 3-6 months down the road.

#2 - Product Inserts

This is the best way to convince your buyers to leave you an Amazon review. A simple message asking them to write a review on Amazon is all it takes to get tens or hundreds of reviews for your product. Now, never ever directly ask for a 5-star review (or a positive review for that matter) since this is against Amazon's terms.

What I like to do instead is put a subtle 5-star images below my product insert after the initial text asking for a feedback.

Here's an example:

[Image 4.2]

Asking them to contact customer service if there's any issue is also one of the best ways to avoid getting a negative review.

****

SELLING ON YOUR OWN WEBSITE

The next step on your progression it to start selling on your own website. So when do you start doing it? When does it make sense to start creating your own mark outside Amazon?

I'd say when these 2 things start happening:

#1 – When you start getting at least 10 sales per day on Amazon

This means your product is a proven hit. You may not be making millions yet but you know that this product has the potential to be a 7-figure product line. You know that this is a proven market because you're getting consistent sales even without spending money on ads.

#2 – When you can already afford to pay for advertisements

I recommend starting with at least $3,000 in ad budget if you're going to advertise outside Amazon.

Don't worry because you don't necessarily have to spend all of it in just one week. In the beginning, the goal is to test things out and breakeven. You can get started with Facebook Ads and then expand to other platforms if you want to scale even more.

What Platform Should You Use?

I recommend that you start with Shopify.

It's easy to use and its monthly membership is pretty affordable.

Prices may differ depending on where you live, but here's the current membership options available in North America.

	Basic Shopify	Shopify	Advanced Shopify
	All the basics for starting a new business	Everything you need for a growing business	Advanced features for scaling your business
Monthly price	$29	$79	$299
SHOPIFY PAYMENTS			
Fraud analysis	✓	✓	✓
Online credit card rates	[illegible]	[illegible]	[illegible]
In-person credit card rates	[illegible]	[illegible]	[illegible]
Additional fees using all payment providers other than Shopify Payments	2.0%	1.0%	0.5%

[Image 4.3]

Keys to a Successful Shopify Store for Beginners

#1 - A Great Product

I hope that you noticed by now that, in my opinion, this is the number 1 thing that all ecommerce business owners should focus on. A great product allows you to sell and even overhype the product as much as you can because you know that it delivers "the goods."

It's easy to be confident in what you are selling when you know that your product works. So always focus on this one first before you even think about any marketing strategies. **A great product IS, bar none the best marketing strategy**. Highlight that, tattoo it in your wrist, I don't care what you do – just don't forget that it's the #1 thing that you should remember from this book.

#2 - Clean Looking Store Theme

Go for more neutral colors and don't overdesign it. I recommend using a combination of 2 colors in addition to white. Go for simple instead of complicated and "award winning" designs. F award winning designs. What does that even mean? Does that mean it makes more money? Or does it mean that a bunch of design nerds who knows nothing about marketing just gathered one evening and voted who has the best designed website… nah, *forgetabouthatcrap.*

Just focus on featuring the product and making sure that you mention its benefits and features. Your website should also be easy to navigate and it shouldn't be *laggy.* One of the most annoying thing that you can experience as a buyer is a slow website. So make sure that you make your site's loading speed is as fast as possible. Just search for "page load optimizer or page speed optimizer" on Shopify's app store and install the highest rated one.

Check out these 2 websites as a great example:

Supply.co – Single Edge Razors
Organifishop.com – Green Juices and Other Health Products

#3 – Paid Advertisements, Then Content Marketing

You don't want to rely on ads in the long term but it is a good way to start introducing your product to the market.

Since you're selling outside Amazon, you have to come up with your own traffic and the fastest way to do that is through paid ads. Once you have ads that are consistently making money every day, then you can start investing some of that profits to your content marketing (which is a long-term play for your business since it's not going to immediately make you any sales in the beginning).

Facebook Ads

FB is probably the easiest ad platform to learn and there's already thousands of free or paid courses available to study. Heck, even just FB's free guide can get you to $1,000 ad spend per day without any problem. You don't have to spend $5,000 with an fb ads guru to learn how to start and scale your ads. Facebook has their own learning platform and you should start with that.

Check out some of these resources to help you get started:

https://www.facebook.com/business/learn

https://www.facebook.com/business/ads-guide

https://neilpatel.com/blog/deep-dive-facebook-advertising/

So what are the keys to making Facebook Ad work for you?

A - Right Targeting

Who are you selling to. You can't say "everyone" because everyone does not exist. *Where do they live? What's the age range? What is their profession? Are they men or women? What things to they like to follow on Facebook? What are their political leanings (left? right?).* All these things add up to an avatar of what a potential buyer would be like. For example, a liberal is more likely to buy anything cat related than a conservative one. Obviously, political affiliations can only get you so much insights and it isn't always applicable without deeper research.

The point is to consider the avatar you are selling to and try to find out as many commonalities about them as possible.

B - Right Images/Videos

I recommend at least an iPhone quality shot or professional photographs that doesn't look like you got it from a stock photo website. Do not use any stock photos because they're eerily perfect and you'll find that your competition might be using them as well.

HOT TIP: Always use PEOPLE in your ad images. They convert better with pretty much any product.

For videos, short previews of the products converts the best. You don't have to start with those million-dollar infomercials. Start with the camera on your phone, shoot different angles of your product + a demo of someone using the product.

C - Longer Testing + One Variable at a Time

Most people spend $500 in 2 days and quit when they didn't get 100% ROI. This is stupid. Spend $10 per day and run 3 different ads with the same everything except for the AD creative/image itself. For example, if I'm selling a single edge razor, I would create 3 ads with the same ad angle, same ad body copy, same targeting and then use 3 different images. I will only test one variable at a time so I'll know which exactly is the factor that affects my ad results the most.

Test at least 3 ads in the beginning and find out the winner within 5-7 days. DO NOT change anything for the first 7 days. DO NOT even touch your ads. Your goal is to let the machine do the work and find out what is the best ad for your product. After the first 7 days, you'll have a clear winner which is obviously the one with the best ROI.

Most of the time, you'll test 3 ads, 2 will probably be at negative ROI and the other one will be at least BREAKEVEN. In this case, breakeven was the winner. Keep running the breakeven ad for another 7 days and let it learn on its own. Most likely, this ad will turn into a winner if you just let it run for an extended amount of time. An ad needs time to learn who the type of person it should target before it starts producing better results. If you're not patient and you're not willing to test, then you won't be able to make Facebook Ads (or any ads for that matter) work for you.

Instagram Marketing

Start with Influencer Marketing

Influencer Marketing is about finding people on social media platforms and then working together to promote your product for you.

I recommend using Buzzsumo's tool for finding influencers on your niche.

https://buzzsumo.com/find-influencers/

Look for micro influencers. 10,000 - 30,000 followers is the best for higher conversion. They are cheaper to work with, and converts higher especially if you pick active ones. Make sure that they're posting at least 2-

3 times per week plus don't forget to look at their profile and see if they are communicating with their followers. If it's just a bunch of semi-nude photos with thirsty men commenting about how hot the influencer is, then just RUN AWAY – fast!

What you want is an influencer who can represent your product in a good light. You want someone who you can work with long-term and build a win-win relationship with.

Here's the price range for influencer at the moment of writing this:

1. An influencer with 10,000 followers could charge $100 per post

2. An influencer with 100,000 followers could charge $1000 per post

3. An influencer with 1,000,000 followers could charge $10,000 per post

https://www.webfx.com/influencer-marketing-pricing.html#instagram-influencer-pricing

Content Marketing

This is more of a long term approach so you shouldn't expect to make thousands of sales from your content marketing efforts – at least not in the first few months.

With content marketing, I recommend that you **don't** start with just 1 platform. I recommend that you start with **1 MEDIUM** instead. Mediums are the way you deliver your content: Is it written? Is it audio? Or is it videos? I recommend that you go heavy on VIDEOS + some photos every now and then.

With videos, you can share them on each and every single one of your platform. You can share them through Facebook, Instagram, YouTube and even your own blog and just add a few text explaining what the video is all about.

What type of video content should you create?

Targeted Topics - look for mini problems that they want to solve along the way. Shoot some instructional videos on how to solve a specific problem by using your product.

Case Studies – you can also show some case studies of customers whose life has been improved because of your product.

Testimonials (Before and After) – people love to see other people getting good results because they imagine that it would happen to them as well. Show some testimonials, preferably with some kind of before and after visuals so they can imagine themselves using your product.

Video is BIG everywhere and you can grow your business faster if you take advantage of it. It's the best way to dominate your market in 2021, 2022 and beyond.

Side Note: If there's a demand (which I can see on the reviews of this book, I'll probably write a marketing guide focusing on this aspect alone).

Additional Resource:

Finding cheap traffic can be hard nowadays. Every big ad platform now are a bit of a pain in the butt to work with. As I was editing this chapter, I discovered an article by Charles Ngo where he talks about finding underpriced sources of traffic and looking for opportunities in the market so you can grow your business.

Check it out here:
https://charlesngo.com/underpricedtraffic/

It doesn't matter whether you're reading it in 2021, 2022 or 2030. The main point is to always be on the lookout for undervalued opportunities and start taking advantage of them as soon as possible.

Chapter 5
How to Scale Your Ecommerce Brand

Taking your business to the next level will require some input that most people just ignore. The truth is, some ecommerce sellers are already satisfied in making $60-100k per year (basically, a full-time income) - and if that's you, then kudos to you and you should enjoy the fruit of your labor. Do what's important to you and do whatever makes you happy. Sometimes, the money we make beyond what we need is just a distraction for living a life that will truly make us fulfilled.

But if you want to expand beyond that, then it will take some more time investment and additional work. The good news is these additional work are doable even for people who doesn't have a huge budget or cashflow yet.

Here are 5 Strategies to Expand to 7-Figures Per Year

#1 - Sell Other Products

When other ecommerce business owners ask me how they can improve their sales and overall, their brand's identity - all I say to them are these 3 words.

SELL OTHER PRODUCTS.

If you think about it, most of the billion dollar brands out there sell multiple products at the same time. Different products solve different needs. So all you have to do is find products that are similar or complementary to what you're already selling.

For example, if you sell razors, then the natural complementary products for that are blades, shaving cream, post shave oil, face wash, and moisturizer. These are the complementary products that matches your original one. If you're selling a quality razor, then they shouldn't need to buy it every week. That means you won't have anything to sell to the customer who already bought your razor if you don't have any of those complementary ones. In addition, remember that it's 5x easier to sell to a current customer than with a new one. In terms of cost per customer acquisition, you won't really need to spend that much to convert your current customers on new product offerings.

Want to expand to 7-figures? Then start selling other products that also adds value to your customers' lives.

#2 - Cart Abandonment

This will depend on what platform you're using so I couldn't give you a specific instruction on how to do this.

I do recommend that you install some kind of automation that emails customers whenever they abandon their cart. Majority of people who click **add to cart** will actually won't proceed to paying the item. This means you're losing hundreds of sales that you could've easily gotten already.

I recommend that you offer a discount or *special offer* to anyone who abandons their cart.

For example, Organifishop.com sends a 3-day email sequence to anyone who abandons their cart and they offer an additional 10% discount to anyone who will continue with the checkout process.

[Image 5.1]

This is a great way to get customers who are on the cusp of purchasing your product but couldn't quite pull the trigger because of some lingering doubt in their minds.

The job of the offer is to make the buying decision easier for them.

To make the offer even better, I recommend that you also put a time-bounded discount link that will expire in 3 days. This makes them act faster and it encourages your customers to make a decision now.

#3 - Raise Your AOV

AOV or your average order value is the total amount you make on average per customer order.

To calculate your company's **average order value**, simply divide your total revenue by the number of **orders**. For example, let's say that in the month of September, your web store's sales was $31,000 and you had a total of 1,000 **orders**. $31,000 divided by 1,000 = $31, so September's monthly **AOV** was $31.

Here's a few things you can do to increase your AOV:

Offer a free shipping threshold... Offer free shipping to anyone who will have an average order value of $75 or more. I recommend offering free shipping to anyone who orders double of what your current AOV is.

Offer other products... The more products for them to add to cart, the higher your AOV could be.

Offer time sensitive deals… Every 4 weeks or so, you can offer some kind of time-sensitive deals for your complementary products.

Upsells… Make sure that you offer different product specifications like colors, specs, and sizes so you can upsell a more expensive version of your products.

Apple is the master of doing this so you should take a look at how they make their offers and upsells.

[Image 5.2]

#4 - Focus on Your Email List

Your email list is your number 1 marketing asset. I would rather have 100,000 people on my list than 2,000,000 Instagram followers. With email, I can reach them directly and I can communicate better due to the nature of how we read emails.

I recommend that you send your customers weekly emails talking about new products, special offers, customer testimonials, a new video that you made and pretty much anything that adds value to your customer.

Here are some resources to check out when it comes to ecommerce email marketing:

https://sleeknote.com/blog/e-commerce-email-marketing

https://www.sendinblue.com/blog/ecommerce-email-strategy/

https://neilpatel.com/blog/bootstrap-e-commerce-sales/

#5 - Scale Through Ads

You should never rely on ads alone but that doesn't mean you shouldn't run them. Ads are still a great source of consistent sales because more people will be seeing your product listing on a consistent basis.

THE ROI WASH APPROACH

Most people think that they have to have hundreds of thousands of dollars already to get started with online ads. Not really, not if your smart enough to implement what I call the ROI WASH APPROACH.

Here's what usually happens when other people run ads online.

#1 – They have some sort of fixed advertising budget.

#2 – They start running ads and they go "all in" – "I'm gonna run this ad till I lose x amount of money [the fixed budget]"

#3 – They lose it all or they lose 25%-50% and they, pardon my French, b*tch about ads being a scam

Here's what you should do instead:

THE ROI WASH APPROACH

THE NUMBERS

Example:

Start with $500, make $400 back… that's a loss.

Re-invest $400 back into ads, this time using better data that you gathered from your initial "loss." Re-adjust you ad strategy and create a better ad or better targeting.

From that $400, you'll probably make $700 back because you now have better and more accurate data for your ads. Even if you're still at the breakeven point or negative ROI, you're now in a better position to run your ads because of you have a more accurate set of data.

Keep re-investing that $700 back…

Let's say that you made $1,000 ($300 profit from that initial $700). Don't go party around and don't buy any fancy stuff. Just re-invest that $1,000 again to the business and just keep growing your treasure chest.

The key is to re-invest your ROI over and over again. It's like washing your ROI, thus it's called the "ROI WASH" method.

THE APPROACH

#1 – Start running small ads just like what I taught you in the FB ads part in chapter 4.

#2 – You'll likely lose 20%-30% of your ad budget but you will still make sales. It's likely that you'll also get to breakeven. The goal in the beginning is to gather data so you can re-adjust your targeting/ad message later.

#3 – Even if you lose 20%-30%, you probably were still able to make some sales. **START RE-INVESTING YOUR SALES INTO YOUR ADS.**

Okay, this is crucial so read this again.

START RE-INVESTING YOUR SALES INTO YOUR ADS. This is how the pros do it. They don't quit when they get negative ROI. They just re-adjust and find what works and they start re-investing their sales into their ads. By doing this, you'll be able to increase that ad budget again and keep testing.

#4 – After you re-adjust your strategy, you'll probably start making positive ROI. Usually, for e-commerce, you'll see that gurus are bragging about 100%-500% ROI. That's crazy and that's not scalable. You should aim for 10%-20% instead since it's a bit more realistic.

#5 – Once you start making that positive ROI, just re-invest that profit back again to the ads. This is how you grow an ad budget and this is how you make money long-term.

Just keep washing that ROI and keep on improving your ads. Eventually, you'll get higher returns and you'll have a sustainable business that gets consistent profits day-in and day-out.

BONUS - Test Those Trinkets

There will always be little things that will help you grow your ecommerce business. Most of the time, you'll have some kind of app that do whatever those little things are. For example, "Referral Candy" allows your customer to share your products and they'll get to have discounts that they can use on your store. It's a win-win. Another one is called "Subscription by Recharge" which allows you to sell products on a subscription basis. There's all kind of apps with different functions and it's your job as an ecommerce business owner to test things out and see if they will work for your own store.

Check out the following link to read more about these apps that you can test for your own store.

https://www.referralcandy.com/blog/best-shopify-apps/

https://www.optimonk.com/shopify-app-store-best-shopify-apps-drive-sales/

Note: Not all of them will have a major impact on your business but it won't hurt to test things out so you'll find out what works for your own brand.

Conclusion

The right action will give you the awesome results you are aiming for. But most people get lost in the process and gets overwhelmed by what they have to do. So here are some quick actionable advice I want to give you before I let you off the hook (*or before you read another one of my books – wink-wink)...*

1 - Decide if this business is for you. By now you already have an idea of how much time, effort and money it takes to start and grow an ecommerce business. There's no shame in realizing that this type of business isn't for you. In fact, I would assume that at least half the people reading this isn't going to do anything about the information they just learned. Another 50% will probably dabble into it and start looking for products, and then 1-2% will actually proceed into selling it on Amazon or on their own websites. If you want to be in that top 1%-2% - then you have to fully commit to it.

2 - Start looking for problems, then start researching product ideas. Focus your attention in trying to solve real-world problems. Start with your own problems and then expand to the people around you. Always be on the lookout for problems that you can solve since these issues may turn into a profitable product idea.

3 - Create a brand identity that makes you excited. Try to create a brand identity that makes you want to work on your business. If your personality is quirky and bubbly, then you may want to incorporate that to your own brand. It's always nice to see founders bring some much needed energy to an ecommerce brand and not just focus on how much money they will make.

4 - Choose a selling platform. You can either start with Amazon or your own website. I always recommend that people start with Amazon because of the free traffic, but if you already have some marketing and advertising skills – then you can go straight to having your own store since you'll have more control over your own brand.

5 - Choose one "customer getting" method. Lastly, you should focus on just one customer acquisition method especially in the beginning. This allows you to get better results [aka more profits], that you can then leverage and re-invest on other parts of your business like customer service, product improvement, faster shipping, and other advertising platforms. Hopefully, I was able to give you some valuable information that you can use in your journey to starting and growing your own brand.

I wish you all the best in this amazing journey,

Red

OTHER FBA BOOKS

AMAZON FBA Step by Step (by Red Mikhail) – to help you get started with Amazon FBA (the basics)

FBA Product Research 101 – an in depth guide to product research

Amazon Keyword Research 101 – an in depth guide to Amazon keyword research

FBA Product Sourcing Blueprint – a step by step blueprint on sourcing products and shipping it to Amazon/your preferred destination

Amazon FBA Sales Boost – 33 little tricks to triple your Amazon sales

These are also available as audiobooks.

You can find the whole series here:

https://www.amazon.com/gp/product/B086QZCJQQ

Review Request

As you might already know, reviews are the lifeblood of every author out there. If you found some value in this one, allow me to humbly ask for a review on Amazon as it does help in spreading my message.

Thank you so much and good luck on building your ecommerce brand.

www.ingramcontent.com/pod-product-compliance
Lightning Source LLC
Chambersburg PA
CBHW021241060726
47590CB00005B/1848